ACRL
UNIVERSITY LIBRARY
STATISTICS
1994-95

A Compilation of Statistics
from One Hundred Sixteen
University Libraries

Compiled at the

Library Research Center
Graduate School of Library and Information Science
University of Illinois at Urbana-Champaign

Project Coordinator

Hugh A. Thompson
Association of College and Research Libraries

Association of College and Research Libraries
A Division of the American Library Association
Chicago, Illinois
1996

ASSOCIATION OF

COLLEGE

& RESEARCH

LIBRARIES

A DIVISION OF THE
AMERICAN LIBRARY ASSOCIATION

Published by the Association of College and Research Libraries
A Division of the American Library Association
50 East Huron Street
Chicago, IL 60611
1-800-545-2433

ISBN 0-8389-7831-2

Printed in the United States of America.

TABLE OF CONTENTS

I. INTRODUCTION

This report marks the ninth time since 1979 that the Association of College and Research Libraries (ACRL) has conducted a biennial statistical study, which this year surveyed 151 universities.

The institutions surveyed are selected according to Carnegie Classifications Research I, Research II, Doctoral Granting I, and Doctoral Granting II. The Association of Research Libraries (ARL) member institutions so classified are surveyed by ARL and are not included in this study. ACRL uses the ARL survey instrument and thanks are extended to ARL for providing it to ACRL.

One hundred sixteen universities reported data for the 1994-95 fiscal year. Data categories include: collections, interlibrary loan, personnel, expenditures, number of Ph.D.s awarded, faculty, and enrollment. Percentages and ratios have also been compiled for various categories.

The Library Research Center (LRC) of the University of Illinois Graduate School of Library and Information Science compiled the statistics for this study and the previous 1992-93 study. Compiler's notes have been provided for clarification on how the data for this report was compiled. Special thanks to Diane LaBarbera, research data analyst, for compiling and analyzing the data. Other LRC staff who are owed thanks include: John Walder, research programmer, who formatted and produced the camera-ready copy; Edward Lakner who managed the project at LRC; and the students Leah Myers and Jack Van Leer, who spent many hours on coding and data entry.

Special thanks are due to the librarians who devote so much time and effort to carefully complete the survey. Thanks to Hugh Thompson, ACRL Program Officer, for coordinating the project.

This edition of the ACRL University Library Statistics, 1994-95 is the ninth in this series which started with 1978-79 data. Other editions reported statistics for 1981-82, 1983-84, 1985-86, 1987-88, 1988-89, 1990-91, and 1992-93.

Althea Jenkins   Patricia M. Kelley
ACRL Executive Director   Chair, ACRL Statistics Committee

The data are available on disk to anyone purchasing this report. They are provided as dbs files in ASCII format. To order, call ACRL Statistics, 800-545-2433 x2519. Please indicate which size disk you need (5.25 or 3.5).

1994-95
ACRL LIBRARY DATA TABLES

ACRL LIBRARY DATA TABLES 1994-95

COLLECTIONS

	Institution	Notes	Volumes in Library	Volumes Added (Gross)	Volumes Added (Net)	Mono-graphs Purchased	Current Serials Purchased	Current Serials Not Purchased	Current Serials Total
	(Survey Question #)		(3)	(2a)	(2c)	(4)	(5)	(6)	(7)
Lib. No.									
1	Akron	LBb+	1,691,709	U/A	31,380	25,655	U/A	0	6,962
2	Alabama, Birmingham	MBGb+	1,064,930	46,551	45,971	13,126	5,014	273	5,287
3	Alaska	b+	992,427	21,179	11,477	U/A	U/A	U/A	6,889
4	American	BGb+	635,767	20,549	18,007	20,549	U/A	U/A	3,091
5	Andrews	Gb+	601,623	11,482	10,321	6,842	U/A	U/A	2,828
6	Arkansas, Fayetteville	LG+	1,452,137	31,696	28,470	16,461	11,170	5,128	16,298
7	Atlanta	Gb+	529,833	13,816	13,816	14,257	1,784	5	1,789
8	Ball State	b+	1,067,498	30,800	13,035	16,819	U/A	U/A	4,956
9	Baylor	LMB+	1,560,980	U/A	29,209	U/A	U/A	U/A	9,424
10	Biola	b+	249,673	5,891	3,883	2,401	922	175	1,097
11	Bowling Green State	Bb+	1,963,805	63,562	60,921	14,113	U/A	U/A	5,343
12	Brandeis	G+	981,911	26,695	25,541	19,891	4,027	2,033	6,060
13	Calgary	LMGb+	U/A	U/A	U/A	U/A	U/A	U/A	14,478
14	Calif. Institute of Tech.	B+	536,913	16,673	16,180	U/A	U/A	U/A	5,119
15	Calif., Santa Cruz	Gb+	1,132,156	36,573	35,194	U/A	U/A	U/A	8,948
16	Carnegie-Mellon	Gb+	873,540	22,305	21,299	U/A	3,335	226	3,561
17	Catholic	b+	1,368,049	30,346	25,899	6,309	9,219	204	9,423
18	Central Florida	b+	781,669	41,114	38,877	U/A	4,671	0	4,671
19	Claremont	BGb+	1,213,831	31,739	25,365	14,471	5,799	230	6,029
20	Clark	b+	520,943	9,266	6,937	6,240	2,298	335	2,633
21	Clarkson	Gb	224,306	6,639	4,358	U/A	2,552	159	2,711
22	Clemson	Gb+	860,260	36,177	34,348	13,989	7,180	3,965	11,145
23	Cleveland State	Gb	901,022	26,504	22,022	13,331	U/A	U/A	3,863
24	Colorado, Denver	Gb+	624,500	19,052	14,190	12,124	U/A	U/A	4,177
25	Colorado School of Mines	+	140,518	3,785	-3,380	1,410	1,457	440	1,897
26	Denver	b+	1,107,670	26,672	19,350	17,827	U/A	U/A	5,330
27	DePaul	BGb+	502,495	22,939	20,741	17,581	4,397	263	4,660
28	Drake	+	475,912	9,072	7,700	8,500	2,900	55	2,955
29	Duquesne	b+	378,724	6,476	-27,266	3,297	1,886	130	2,016
30	East Texas State	BGb+	700,251	8,438	8,280	5,899	U/A	U/A	1,975
31	Florida Atlantic	B+	638,071	28,187	26,609	6,286	U/A	U/A	4,056
32	Fordham	LBGb+	1,613,828	27,761	21,207	16,712	U/A	U/A	11,307
33	George Mason	LBb+	671,528	40,582	37,564	30,769	9,246	287	9,533
34	George Washington	BGb+	1,352,922	30,180	28,704	17,840	9,417	1,092	10,509
35	Georgia State	Lb+	1,245,668	35,158	30,271	26,482	9,909	1,189	11,098
36	Hahnemann	MGb+	197,153	7,968	4,477	2,209	U/A	U/A	2,912
37	Hofstra	L+	1,099,900	U/A	18,777	17,369	U/A	U/A	2,786
38	Idaho		847,233	29,974	27,850	10,000	5,526	5,425	10,951
39	Idaho State	MBb	522,064	11,866	11,373	7,039	3,209	93	3,302
40	Illinois State		1,279,887	30,584	21,038	16,390	4,725	677	5,402

+ - See Footnotes   G - Government Documents not included in Serials Count   U/A - Unavailable
L - Includes Law Library   B - Includes Branch Campuses   N/A - Not Applicable
M - Includes Medical Library   b - Bibliographic Count

ACRL LIBRARY DATA TABLES 1994-95

COLLECTIONS

Microform Units	Government Documents	Computer Files	Archives and Manus.	Carto-graphic Materials	Graphic Materials	Audio Materials	Film and Video	
(8)	(9)	(10)	(11)	(12)	(13)	(14)	(15)	(Survey Question #)
								Institution
1,686,820	U/A	U/A	20,000	U/A	U/A	U/A	36,487	Akron
1,156,575	0	349	349	145	37,916	9,990	1,469	Alabama, Birmingham
992,228	197,631	205	10,305	19,242	515,125	10,143	6,085	Alaska
858,300	U/A	500	2,875	68	318	24,304	4,311	American
530,750	N/A	U/A	563	43,367	U/A	20,823	49,211	Andrews
2,649,581	627,514	U/A	7,803	109,952	U/A	16,456	861	Arkansas, Fayetteville
641,724	N/A	3,415	63,805	1,625	3,885	695	4,095	Atlanta
836,556	10,031	3,274	4,405	142,922	316,301	31,825	10,844	Ball State
1,091,804	570,556	1,610	4,066	14,373	79,998	42,445	4,060	Baylor
407,022	N/A	15	450	U/A	N/A	N/A	N/A	Biola
2,070,934	374,520	738	5,728	2,971	U/A	629,684	17,312	Bowling Green State
834,668	371,255	212	1,158	6	11,122	23,166	6,174	Brandeis
3,134,056	U/A	80	6,780	1,094,304	U/A	41,286	U/A	Calgary
536,907	109,245	228	U/A	U/A	U/A	3,321	345	Calif. Institute of Tech.
709,462	82,608	1,280	U/A	168,418	275,167	24,557	5,470	Calif., Santa Cruz
809,527	0	1,915	4,132	157	189,799	21,867	4,549	Carnegie-Mellon
1,237,338	0	0	10,726	0	0	21,589	13,228	Catholic
1,713,464	66,800	1,251	10,016	3,293	1,303	5,950	2,886	Central Florida
1,278,959	717,830	842	5,764	U/A	U/A	U/A	475	Claremont
60,000	N/A	83	1,600	208,188	N/A	450	621	Clark
269,289	0	660	309	419	39	1,043	613	Clarkson
1,075,981	599,083	1,080	8,867	20,892	87,314	670	530	Clemson
638,325	0	331	2,360	57,472	13,635	21,638	3,923	Cleveland State
1,079,112	0	806	1,750	9,165	22,916	15,341	4,283	Colorado, Denver
1,082,566	377,910	500	666	224,376	0	0	17	Colorado School of Mines
912,115	744,077	1,376	5,754	U/A	U/A	U/A	U/A	Denver
501,313	U/A	1,378	1,208	U/A	65,664	10,312	4,301	DePaul
710,000	89,758	120	350	0	0	0	10	Drake
68,208	U/A	647	U/A	U/A	6,582	5,488	305	Duquesne
866,551	414,469	482	1,050	139	22,136	5,272	0	East Texas State
3,279,194	271,212	265	120	30,693	8,705	8,562	6,850	Florida Atlantic
2,010,409	355,480	614	2,303	N/A	N/A	N/A	1,116	Fordham
1,864,737	280,234	2,016	4,513	212,712	211	10,846	4,729	George Mason
1,342,696	0	615	9,671	14,617	143,811	10,753	5,125	George Washington
2,027,368	745,932	1,326	5,747	8,043	193,181	63,654	4,297	Georgia State
3	0	653	2,750	0	720	2,227	2,150	Hahnemann
2,167,850	229,925	885	1,209	67,675	2,900	2,833	5,190	Hofstra
1,176,725	550,238	853	5,575	187,384	103,009	2,765	47	Idaho
1,736,824	422,640	460	1,025	42,884	100	100	3,000	Idaho State
1,865,148	380,854	836	1,610	469,270	29,205	22,192	3,888	Illinois State

U/A - Unavailable   N/A - Not Applicable

ACRL LIBRARY DATA TABLES 1994-95

COLLECTIONS

Lib. No.	Institution	Notes	Volumes in Library (3)	Volumes Added (Gross) (2a)	Volumes Added (Net) (2c)	Mono-graphs Purchased (4)	Current Serials Purchased (5)	Current Serials Not Purchased (6)	Current Serials Total (7)
41	Indiana/Purdue, Indianapolis	B+	363,285	29,943	22,452	U/A	3,946	562	4,508
42	Indiana State	+	1,209,617	37,226	29,487	U/A	5,170	337	5,507
43	Kansas State	B+	1,340,443	32,784	32,784	14,986	6,621	2,229	8,850
44	La Sierra	b	225,311	2,993	1,520	2,993	1,156	266	1,422
45	Lehigh	Gb+	1,105,636	34,768	28,337	11,929	5,340	1,800	7,140
46	Louisiana Tech	+	359,895	6,875	4,508	3,656	2,635	0	2,635
47	Louisville	LMb+	1,315,284	84,721	82,339	U/A	U/A	U/A	12,812
48	Loyola, Chicago	LMBb+	1,407,134	62,956	58,036	29,271	U/A	U/A	11,789
49	Maine, Orono	Bb+	873,431	24,767	19,017	15,181	6,150	250	6,400
50	Marquette	LG+	1,074,199	41,000	35,699	22,768	8,074	828	8,902
51	Maryland, Baltimore Ct.	Gb+	610,164	17,735	17,735	U/A	U/A	U/A	4,067
52	Memphis State	BGb+	1,010,046	7,868	7,341	U/A	5,601	4,100	9,701
53	Miami, Ohio	+	1,563,098	98,615	96,171	22,913	U/A	U/A	6,014
54	Michigan Technological	Gb	795,312	15,091	9,045	2,214	6,260	2,895	9,155
55	Middle Tennessee State	G	604,017	17,170	12,341	17,170	U/A	U/A	3,507
56	Mississippi	BG+	797,387	17,609	17,609	U/A	11,786	N/A	11,786
57	Missouri, Kansas City	LMGb+	962,529	25,178	20,413	10,187	U/A	U/A	8,793
58	Missouri, Rolla	Gb+	455,302	8,144	4,683	3,372	1,190	266	1,456
59	Missouri, St. Louis	G+	612,621	14,520	13,821	6,877	3,300	5,863	9,163
60	Montana State	b	574,602	6,122	4,736	3,979	3,704	783	4,487
61	Montreal	LMGb+	2,196,734	60,972	58,287	26,194	U/A	U/A	19,270
62	Nevada, Reno	MBb+	911,567	31,045	17,919	12,354	6,268	8,823	15,091
63	New Brunswick	BGb+	1,085,567	19,106	17,946	8,571	3,969	943	4,912
64	New Hampshire	b+	1,059,055	23,826	22,051	8,815	5,885	16	5,901
65	New Mexico State	b+	973,265	23,860	19,913	11,898	5,882	1,446	7,328
66	New Orleans	Gb+	614,985	14,413	14,028	4,267	3,205	2,750	5,955
67	New School	Gb+	247,943	6,552	5,950	6,480	1,215	15	1,230
68	North Carolina, Greensboro	b+	876,640	28,638	25,119	28,390	4,978	451	5,429
69	North Dakota State	Gb+	483,458	17,641	15,225	3,345	3,836	3,346	7,182
70	North Texas	BG+	1,153,273	16,650	16,650	16,650	U/A	U/A	8,858
71	Northeastern	Bb+	808,509	33,549	31,257	26,289	8,594	369	8,963
72	Northern Arizona	G	550,014	23,627	20,294	21,853	U/A	U/A	6,649
73	Northern Colorado	b+	645,121	18,034	5,605	8,189	U/A	U/A	3,710
74	Northern Illinois	LBGb+	1,525,438	35,167	31,457	15,484	9,434	6,362	15,796
75	Ohio	MBGb+	1,992,066	49,552	45,188	U/A	U/A	U/A	25,564
76	Old Dominion	G+	557,561	15,549	11,937	U/A	U/A	U/A	6,905
77	Ottawa	LMBb+	1,479,046	35,787	-785	18,291	U/A	U/A	9,861
78	Pacific	b+	440,148	8,070	2,406	8,070	2,480	200	2,680
79	Pepperdine	BG+	339,460	8,529	5,421	2,594	U/A	U/A	3,186
80	Polytechnic	B+	197,300	609	609	600	U/A	U/A	821

+ - See Footnotes
L - Includes Law Library
M - Includes Medical Library

G - Government Documents not included in Serials Count
B - Includes Branch Campuses
b - Bibliographic Count

U/A - Unavailable
N/A - Not Applicable

4

COLLECTIONS

Microform Units	Government Documents	Computer Files	Archives and Manus.	Carto-graphic Materials	Graphic Materials	Audio Materials	Film and Video	
(8)	(9)	(10)	(11)	(12)	(13)	(14)	(15)	(Survey Question #)
								Institution
1,008,114	80,404	32,810	U/A	3,785	430,364	131	2,895	Indiana/Purdue, Indianapolis
889,864	0	508	120	U/A	U/A	U/A	U/A	Indiana State
2,431,669	1,340,858	374	7,225	23,781	31,465	17,143	2,009	Kansas State
315,417	0	0	N/A	U/A	U/A	2,523	558	La Sierra
1,658,580	177,289	1,147	158	4,950	17,100	22,320	3,185	Lehigh
1,734,961	706,818	1,383	3,049	30,442	9,875	4,825	9,390	Louisiana Tech
1,621,550	U/A	601	24,253	17,621	2,000,000	15,873	3,081	Louisville
1,246,450	91,753	202	4,137	271	17,245	9,382	5,151	Loyola, Chicago
1,327,178	1,942,950	1,200	3,500	68,000	15,000	11,000	1,200	Maine, Orono
889,055	0	251	13,126	0	0	389	1,546	Marquette
854,735	148,225	U/A	853	5,321	1,434,185	28,694	2,680	Maryland, Baltimore Ct.
2,871,546	458,345	306	3,476	46,438	762,490	21,357	5,904	Memphis State
2,662,636	535,060	321	U/A	101,859	7,622	17,238	1,180	Miami, Ohio
440,508	0	892	U/A	127,349	U/A	209	86	Michigan Technological
1,116,512	U/A	U/A	U/A	U/A	U/A	U/A	U/A	Middle Tennessee State
983,561	2,090,997	1,660	36,231	U/A	U/A	17,980	23,956	Mississippi
1,813,413	502,969	1,020	N/A	75	148,224	295,192	3,328	Missouri, Kansas City
509,889	66,051	973	N/A	72,006	500	3,141	896	Missouri, Rolla
1,908,246	361,663	1,463	7,567	U/A	U/A	448	407	Missouri, St. Louis
1,333,061	U/A	536	13,190	22,700	79,962	679	998	Montana State
1,390,557	0	173	N/A	691	113,424	26,048	10,532	Montreal
2,975,375	1,284,632	1,022	6,670	136,470	199,296	23,912	5,783	Nevada, Reno
2,955,623	0	1,157	4,744	46,630	59,750	2,345	800	New Brunswick
866,478	1,459,576	444	3,000	126,480	N/A	10,435	2,604	New Hampshire
956,989	471,062	21	10,890	23,051	N/A	880	121	New Mexico State
2,069,860	321,878	1,072	13,753	31,038	N/A	19,733	513	New Orleans
20,703	U/A	6	458	0	119,921	7,349	0	New School
1,110,219	258,406	766	1,630	15,971	10,280	9,369	45	North Carolina, Greensboro
345,759	243,046	491	2,000	90,018	56,032	1,880	363	North Dakota State
2,828,456	369,562	1,722	4,186	18,267	39,669	47,149	6,829	North Texas
1,879,678	172,091	731	3,288	4,597	429	8,433	7,137	Northeastern
369,727	395,058	1,263	2,768	35,071	753,000	17,133	6,412	Northern Arizona
1,012,488	411,435	959	1,500	46,471	20,027	32,784	4,661	Northern Colorado
2,660,060	1,227,826	U/A	5,428	215,686	1,213	36,870	U/A	Northern Illinois
2,321,171	0	2,737	9,197	164,927	96,278	46,368	58,513	Ohio
450,605	159,480	37	U/A	U/A	U/A	38,486	11	Old Dominion
1,368,610	774,352	814	458	405,355	211,268	14,414	5,953	Ottawa
556,534	3,500	30	3,023	U/A	50,718	19,994	1,091	Pacific
399,575	N/A	U/A	849	U/A	U/A	3,667	649	Pepperdine
56,628	0	289	408	0	0	0	200	Polytechnic

U/A - Unavailable   N/A - Not Applicable

ACRL LIBRARY DATA TABLES 1994-95

COLLECTIONS

Lib. No.	Institution	Notes	Volumes in Library	Volumes Added (Gross)	Volumes Added (Net)	Mono-graphs Purchased	Current Serials Purchased	Current Serials Not Purchased	Current Serials Total
	(Survey Question #)		(3)	(2a)	(2c)	(4)	(5)	(6)	(7)
81	Portland State	G+	981,391	24,251	23,319	21,611	8,028	3,271	11,299
82	Puerto Rico		1,367,167	51,195	42,421	8,600	5,931	983	6,914
83	Rhode Island	BGb+	1,057,197	19,368	18,476	5,447	5,751	8,065	13,816
84	Rockefeller	b	182,249	2,631	-1,455	856	453	11	464
85	SUNY, Binghamton	b+	1,544,905	48,037	39,488	34,429	8,897	403	9,300
86	SUNY Coll. Env. Sci. & For.	Gb+	115,488	3,384	1,090	1,194	1,146	638	1,784
87	San Diego State	b+	1,121,934	29,415	26,353	15,268	4,990	700	5,690
88	San Francisco	Bb+	603,341	18,248	14,382	12,820	2,187	194	2,381
89	South Dakota	b+	460,749	10,133	8,895	6,467	2,252	445	2,697
90	South Dakota State	b+	501,767	14,116	12,982	12,982	3,024	473	3,497
91	South Florida	MB+	1,524,685	46,646	44,085	33,522	8,372	385	8,757
92	Southern Methodist	LGb+	2,273,228	46,270	39,078	19,842	5,759	461	6,220
93	Southern Mississippi	b+	877,109	5,098	5,098	4,447	4,546	434	4,980
94	Southwestern Louisiana	Gb+	717,776	16,542	16,092	6,782	5,300	587	5,887
95	St. John's	LBGb+	1,202,376	38,977	34,006	32,494	13,351	1,820	15,171
96	St. Louis	LMB+	1,403,861	38,503	32,338	14,226	12,457	1,377	13,834
97	Stevens Inst. of Tech.	+	106,288	1,804	1,686	902	U/A	U/A	140
98	Teachers College	b+	557,404	10,555	9,985	1,570	2,203	13	2,216
99	Tennessee Tech	b+	400,565	12,891	9,650	U/A	3,673	509	4,182
100	Texas, Arlington	Gb+	957,936	34,831	28,188	4,503	U/A	U/A	7,908
101	Texas, Dallas	B+	554,547	29,978	29,589	U/A	U/A	U/A	3,811
102	Texas Woman's	Bb+	794,455	12,177	6,184	3,486	2,591	106	2,697
103	Toledo	Bb+	868,378	26,886	23,543	U/A	4,942	105	5,047
104	Tufts	b	607,816	24,038	21,227	24,038	2,396	188	2,584
105	Tulsa	LGb+	790,276	18,453	11,859	8,314	6,962	1,321	8,283
106	U.S. International	+	196,934	2,900	1,316	U/A	U/A	U/A	971
107	Utah State	G+	1,261,463	74,606	44,345	7,890	4,667	9,343	14,010
108	Vermont	Mb+	1,153,752	32,960	25,764	U/A	U/A	U/A	17,136
109	Virginia Commonwealth	MGb+	1,130,562	53,218	46,767	33,329	7,717	2,069	9,786
110	Wake Forest	LMB+	1,276,536	40,238	37,793	25,568	U/A	U/A	14,891
111	Wichita State	BG+	993,724	22,576	21,608	14,433	3,228	10,024	13,252
112	William and Mary	LBb+	1,277,308	44,271	36,994	20,465	9,424	1,789	11,213
113	Windsor	LBb+	2,188,943	U/A	U/A	12,098	U/A	U/A	493,886
114	Wisconsin, Milwaukee	Gb+	1,897,378	41,515	36,382	18,536	U/A	U/A	7,950
115	Wyoming	b+	1,134,211	29,072	22,177	5,094	U/A	U/A	12,150
116	Yeshiva	LMBGb+	1,013,674	U/A	18,362	U/A	U/A	U/A	10,176

+ - See Footnotes
L - Includes Law Library
M - Includes Medical Library

G - Government Documents not included in Serials Count
B - Includes Branch Campuses
b - Bibliographic Count

U/A - Unavailable
N/A - Not Applicable

ACRL LIBRARY DATA TABLES 1994-95

COLLECTIONS

Microform Units	Government Documents	Computer Files	Archives and Manus.	Carto-graphic Materials	Graphic Materials	Audio Materials	Film and Video	
(8)	(9)	(10)	(11)	(12)	(13)	(14)	(15)	(Survey Question #)
								Institution
2,136,893	455,751	4,760	11,145	52,979	74,935	22,726	4,277	Portland State
1,665,365	U/A	169	54,446	20,241	132,017	28,299	1,066	Puerto Rico
1,448,733	677,374	1,018	9,746	15,175	149,001	2,159	4,775	Rhode Island
20	1,589	0	0	0	0	0	5	Rockefeller
1,471,103	381,463	614	541	122,255	0	113,390	416	SUNY, Binghamton
153,748	0	12	735	109	40	1,092	548	SUNY Coll. Env. Sci. & For.
3,738,123	592,474	245	4,812	173,572	428,214	214,107	1,872	San Diego State
653,769	243,474	234	510	1,625	U/A	268	713	San Francisco
569,698	275,275	365	3,527	23,926	1,095	6,272	2,730	South Dakota
744,653	344,212	1,920	200	U/A	U/A	3,193	U/A	South Dakota State
3,194,132	533,729	477	6,975	84,290	100,955	36,279	16,909	South Florida
1,562,468	U/A	791	3,341	211,452	340,875	22,800	4,812	Southern Methodist
2,265,196	966,727	83	7,810	4,587	733	8,950	5,516	Southern Mississippi
1,745,804	160,881	772	2,256	4,924	U/A	5,474	36	Southwestern Louisiana
2,401,059	1,000	669	1,961	1,050	5,966	10,071	1,908	St. John's
1,276,539	308,621	1,175	2,891	116,978	74,451	4,368	1,098	St. Louis
12,400	U/A	1,450	U/A	N/A	N/A	N/A	N/A	Stevens Inst. of Tech.
483,631	N/A	958	4,740	109	93,000	3,900	2,274	Teachers College
1,127,711	136,004	1,305	3,570	56,607	1,235	6,146	4,733	Tennessee Tech
1,478,656	U/A	527	4,620	44,011	448,992	U/A	U/A	Texas, Arlington
1,524,008	U/A	146	U/A	30,835	U/A	U/A	2,532	Texas, Dallas
1,387,220	N/A	51	2,113	0	3,579	7,925	77,086	Texas Woman's
1,530,334	704,138	286	3,687	150,568	1,351	8,866	3,277	Toledo
862,224	452,631	0	0	107	5,038	13,695	8,488	Tufts
2,416,604	479,067	584	2,792	U/A	288	8,332	1,877	Tulsa
41,131	0	0	0	0	0	0	0	U.S. International
2,134,223	5,407	4,067	7,868	97,415	443,872	17,251	7,769	Utah State
1,470,155	1,047,513	654	9,035	208,939	212,164	10,920	5,926	Vermont
2,452,650	264,611	410	3,602	6,500	51,235	19,698	6,613	Virginia Commonwealth
1,602,327	161,990	1,334	2,603	287	5,708	6,284	3,973	Wake Forest
1,024,262	502,216	83	1,776	754	10,811	13,552	764	Wichita State
1,882,891	552,595	691	8,200	21,971	U/A	16,723	5,013	William and Mary
775,828	350,000	U/A	894	63,500	U/A	U/A	U/A	Windsor
1,495,169	219,282	546	7,000	671,840	166,761	20,991	2,527	Wisconsin, Milwaukee
2,720,746	969,334	U/A	N/A	162,475	N/A	N/A	2,914	Wyoming
1,117,676	26,048	175	2,209	467	U/A	3,617	844	Yeshiva

U/A - Unavailable   N/A - Not Applicable

ACRL LIBRARY DATA TABLES 1994-95

SUMMARY DATA: COLLECTIONS

	Volumes in Library	Volumes Added (Gross)	Volumes Added (Net)	Mono-graphs Purchased	Current Serials Purchased	Current Serials Not Purchased	Current Serials Total
(Survey Question #)	(3)	(2a)	(2c)	(4)	(5)	(6)	(7)
High	2,273,228	98,615	96,171	34,429	13,351	10,024	493,886
Mean	913,888	25,921	21,619	13,077	5,172	1,548	11,171
Median	876,640	23,949	20,104	12,587	4,942	461	5,985
Low	106,288	609	-27,266	600	453	0	140
Total	105,097,142	2,851,295	2,464,613	1,229,231	377,569	112,998	1,295,836
Libraries Reporting	115	110	114	94	73	73	116

ACRL LIBRARY DATA TABLES 1994-95

SUMMARY DATA: COLLECTIONS

Microform Units	Government Documents	Computer Files	Archives and Manus.	Carto-graphic Materials	Graphic Materials	Audio Materials	Film and Video	
(8)	(9)	(10)	(11)	(12)	(13)	(14)	(15)	(Survey Question #)
3,738,123	2,090,997	32,810	63,805	1,094,304	2,000,000	629,684	77,086	High
1,333,537	373,247	1,112	5,841	76,182	136,103	24,859	5,498	Mean
1,207,032	280,234	631	3,409	22,700	22,916	10,228	2,891	Median
3	0	0	0	0	0	0	0	Low
154,690,278	35,458,494	117,852	584,102	7,389,641	11,568,715	2,585,368	582,815	Total
116	95	106	100	97	85	104	106	Libraries Reporting

ACRL LIBRARY DATA TABLES 1994-95

EXPENDITURES

Lib. No.	Institution	Notes	Monographs (16)	Current Serials (17)	Other Library Materials (18)	Misc. Materials (19)	Total Library Materials (20)	Contract Binding (21)
	(Survey Question #)							
1	Akron	LBb+	1,002,086	1,531,592	U/A	U/A	2,533,678	73,099
2	Alabama, Birmingham	MBb+	594,949	1,773,868	106,915	0	2,475,732	116,391
3	Alaska	b+	U/A	478,687	295,089	272,320	1,046,096	5,860
4	American	Bb+	447,700	731,762	107,563	0	1,287,025	32,734
5	Andrews	b+	365,177	240,516	U/A	34,417	640,110	29,300
6	Arkansas, Fayetteville	L+	662,866	2,001,158	208,820	211,438	3,084,282	66,498
7	Atlanta	b+	956,932	585,795	38,193	1,580,920	3,161,840	0
8	Ball State	b+	532,903	877,883	267,562	2,800	1,681,148	80,054
9	Baylor	LMB+	921,480	867,339	434,054	0	2,222,873	76,405
10	Biola	b+	88,060	146,701	25,664	0	260,425	5,797
11	Bowling Green State	Bb+	896,939	1,152,108	28,706	24,450	2,102,203	57,813
12	Brandeis	+	721,951	1,134,516	87,896	191,159	2,135,522	77,249
13	Calgary	LMb+	656,567	1,998,259	U/A	U/A	2,654,827	54,379
14	Calif. Institute of Tech.	B+	199,427	1,679,033	U/A	U/A	1,878,460	64,389
15	Calif., Santa Cruz	b+	944,673	1,436,857	67,027	17,119	2,465,676	132,279
16	Carnegie-Mellon	b+	501,948	1,156,510	177,805	16,481	1,852,744	65,491
17	Catholic	b+	352,446	702,830	48,000	0	1,103,276	42,000
18	Central Florida	b+	1,786,248	1,142,187	U/A	0	2,928,435	103,581
19	Claremont	Bb+	670,888	1,203,256	21,871	320,916	2,216,931	61,033
20	Clark	b+	218,951	466,724	47,616	0	733,291	61,017
21	Clarkson	b	61,474	474,086	90,822	19,249	645,631	2,046
22	Clemson	b+	331,636	1,903,020	U/A	0	2,234,656	65,779
23	Cleveland State	b	261,544	1,219,923	U/A	64,403	1,545,870	44,004
24	Colorado, Denver	b+	405,185	859,809	14,942	30,000	1,309,936	24,478
25	Colorado School of Mines	+	74,931	530,695	838	2,032	608,496	8,788
26	Denver	b+	743,106	823,032	66,657	0	1,632,795	39,780
27	DePaul	Bb+	683,972	986,635	U/A	0	1,670,607	44,827
28	Drake	+	124,347	514,459	66,481	0	705,287	33,276
29	Duquesne	b+	271,372	357,746	63,252	421,476	1,113,846	18,951
30	East Texas State	Bb+	139,331	305,342	35,325	119,632	599,630	17,309
31	Florida Atlantic	B+	437,117	717,571	34,807	791,573	1,981,068	35,732
32	Fordham	LBb+	828,533	1,379,709	325,585	N/A	2,533,827	116,023
33	George Mason	LBb+	1,235,826	1,807,668	562,992	50,278	3,656,764	74,629
34	George Washington	Bb+	814,662	1,639,923	0	232,898	2,687,483	64,961
35	Georgia State	Lb+	1,715,735	1,734,759	388,243	N/A	3,838,737	56,976
36	Hahnemann	Mb+	279,458	803,804	U/A	191,515	1,274,777	41,337
37	Hofstra	L+	644,192	932,590	275,572	3,800	1,856,154	68,608
38	Idaho		282,366	1,129,503	3,688	18,470	1,434,027	59,388
39	Idaho State	MBb	264,054	688,063	40,732	40,000	1,032,849	49,905
40	Illinois State		629,004	1,049,977	196,679	50,604	1,926,264	78,294

+ - See Footnotes   B - Includes Branch Campuses   U/A - Unavailable
L - Includes Law Library   M - Includes Medical Library   N/A - Not Applicable

ACRL LIBRARY DATA TABLES 1994-95

EXPENDITURES

Salaries & Wages Professional Staff	Salaries & Wages Support Staff	Salaries & Wages Student Assistants	Total Salaries & Wages	Other Operating Expend.	Total Library Expend.	
(22)	(23)	(24)	(25)	(26)	(27)	(Survey Question #)
						Institution
1,451,057	903,086	343,037	2,697,180	686,019	5,989,976	Akron
1,419,205	1,182,184	289,385	2,890,774	1,406,341	6,889,238	Alabama, Birmingham
1,425,856	1,049,530	391,458	2,866,844	1,800,757	5,719,557	Alaska
971,173	883,576	244,758	2,099,507	918,177	4,337,443	American
469,738	397,418	211,054	1,078,210	156,031	1,903,651	Andrews
1,384,101	1,024,853	225,996	2,634,950	511,697	6,297,427	Arkansas, Fayetteville
733,274	749,190	160,950	1,643,414	0	4,805,254	Atlanta
1,498,925	1,713,963	374,342	3,587,230	920,946	6,269,378	Ball State
1,249,195	1,244,819	361,919	2,855,933	687,190	5,842,401	Baylor
181,563	160,642	69,272	411,477	98,085	775,784	Biola
1,948,524	1,463,469	308,886	3,720,879	787,789	6,668,684	Bowling Green State
1,044,417	654,090	267,416	1,965,923	419,569	4,598,263	Brandeis
1,429,232	3,074,380	274,880	4,778,492	535,608	8,023,307	Calgary
750,419	1,006,960	21,283	1,778,662	670,052	4,391,563	Calif. Institute of Tech.
1,397,350	1,997,485	534,482	3,929,317	2,143,031	8,670,303	Calif., Santa Cruz
1,229,766	1,051,808	249,622	2,531,196	888,104	5,337,535	Carnegie-Mellon
938,016	622,004	218,005	1,778,025	630,671	3,553,972	Catholic
U/A	U/A	U/A	2,520,120	537,955	6,090,091	Central Florida
768,016	1,026,451	199,120	1,993,587	361,767	4,633,318	Claremont
397,100	266,858	124,137	788,095	152,584	1,734,987	Clark
186,350	136,137	66,062	388,549	151,203	1,187,429	Clarkson
1,081,356	1,181,218	125,194	2,387,768	1,113,497	5,801,700	Clemson
907,693	759,551	305,583	1,972,827	110,484	3,673,186	Cleveland State
1,211,641	1,893,977	180,222	3,285,840	579,169	5,199,423	Colorado, Denver
224,346	289,214	64,685	578,245	217,724	1,413,253	Colorado School of Mines
627,943	558,979	108,415	1,295,337	347,041	3,314,953	Denver
1,241,488	592,750	215,344	2,060,582	577,771	4,353,787	DePaul
418,989	249,169	111,749	779,907	208,860	1,727,330	Drake
507,802	33,259	79,460	620,521	0	1,753,318	Duquesne
543,536	329,190	183,544	1,056,270	59,558	1,732,767	East Texas State
847,050	813,830	88,870	1,749,750	318,676	4,085,226	Florida Atlantic
1,525,060	1,203,186	276,324	3,004,570	726,214	6,380,634	Fordham
1,190,155	901,144	352,721	2,444,020	1,083,426	7,258,839	George Mason
938,013	2,110,868	302,228	3,351,109	1,321,311	7,424,864	George Washington
1,537,916	1,527,676	372,280	3,437,872	1,051,353	8,384,938	Georgia State
988,635	185,860	47,020	1,221,515	269,252	2,806,881	Hahnemann
1,813,883	1,384,574	121,488	3,319,945	386,123	5,630,830	Hofstra
1,491,968	U/A	186,539	1,678,507	404,234	3,576,156	Idaho
520,446	587,055	178,743	1,286,244	112,359	2,481,357	Idaho State
1,613,507	1,573,137	279,084	3,465,728	251,539	5,721,825	Illinois State

U/A - Unavailable   N/A - Not Applicable

EXPENDITURES

Lib. No.	Institution	Notes	Monographs (16)	Current Serials (17)	Other Library Materials (18)	Misc. Materials (19)	Total Library Materials (20)	Contract Binding (21)
	(Survey Question #)							
41	Indiana/Purdue, Indianapolis	B+	661,917	912,574	42,025	280,789	1,897,305	59,904
42	Indiana State	+	453,012	782,646	136,722	0	1,372,380	47,298
43	Kansas State	B+	799,624	1,772,022	36,126	N/A	2,607,772	84,000
44	La Sierra	b	118,144	129,496	U/A	N/A	247,640	23,112
45	Lehigh	b+	549,130	1,634,510	199,758	141,456	2,524,854	55,760
46	Louisiana Tech	+	103,100	594,065	33,205	0	730,370	35,500
47	Louisville	LMb+	1,007,138	2,616,138	301,032	0	3,924,308	87,042
48	Loyola, Chicago	LMBb+	1,323,416	2,221,667	574,363	0	4,119,446	112,535
49	Maine, Orono	Bb+	600,000	1,760,000	61,300	0	2,421,300	66,500
50	Marquette	L+	1,062,864	1,974,432	42,667	102,502	3,182,465	66,964
51	Maryland, Baltimore Ct.	b+	442,953	1,165,282	18,651	25,289	1,652,175	39,822
52	Memphis State	Bb+	337,529	1,582,616	93,644	0	2,013,789	45,788
53	Miami, Ohio	+	783,944	1,219,291	257,339	0	2,260,574	78,516
54	Michigan Technological	b	88,357	988,348	56,240	0	1,132,945	10,768
55	Middle Tennessee State		771,985	854,187	U/A	U/A	1,626,172	40,138
56	Mississippi	B+	620,300	1,409,247	57,521	N/A	2,087,068	35,706
57	Missouri, Kansas City	LMb+	425,936	814,584	144,774	28,912	1,414,206	42,793
58	Missouri, Rolla	b+	275,036	478,233	173,274	0	926,543	20,835
59	Missouri, St. Louis	+	241,997	910,759	51,474	95,437	1,299,667	28,711
60	Montana State	b	110,019	1,191,820	7,667	0	1,309,506	27,077
61	Montreal	LMb+	1,170,574	3,215,682	U/A	0	4,386,256	113,078
62	Nevada, Reno	MBb+	952,658	1,490,615	U/A	U/A	2,443,273	60,514
63	New Brunswick	Bb+	311,028	817,435	U/A	10,874	1,139,337	36,179
64	New Hampshire	b+	155,234	2,133,047	U/A	20,779	2,309,060	32,927
65	New Mexico State	b+	342,977	1,302,026	65,181	0	1,710,184	85,000
66	New Orleans	b+	248,071	795,918	79,299	0	1,123,288	40,243
67	New School	b+	143,160	120,054	32,294	395,671	691,179	25,445
68	North Carolina, Greensboro	b+	769,266	980,000	U/A	50,000	1,799,266	30,000
69	North Dakota State	b+	155,332	848,670	30,862	2,002	1,036,866	14,473
70	North Texas	B+	228,377	1,099,574	338,300	15,256	1,681,507	43,602
71	Northeastern	Bb+	1,181,873	2,181,033	61,746	133,719	3,558,371	156,376
72	Northern Arizona		993,737	903,150	483,106	0	2,379,993	95,786
73	Northern Colorado	b+	294,326	617,558	94,374	185,517	1,191,775	22,059
74	Northern Illinois	LBb+	613,311	2,053,889	322,869	270,214	3,260,283	74,835
75	Ohio	MBb+	1,267,374	1,722,326	124,721	0	3,114,421	86,495
76	Old Dominion	+	540,944	1,009,576	112,867	78,123	1,741,510	51,089
77	Ottawa	LMBb+	560,380	2,185,782	N/A	87,544	2,833,706	75,395
78	Pacific	b+	253,158	418,926	40,934	0	713,018	10,000
79	Pepperdine	B+	114,275	456,650	34,765	193,788	799,478	23,188
80	Polytechnic	B+	56,100	285,550	75,453	0	417,103	0

+ - See Footnotes   B - Includes Branch Campuses   U/A - Unavailable
L - Includes Law Library   M - Includes Medical Library   N/A - Not Applicable

ACRL LIBRARY DATA TABLES 1994-95

EXPENDITURES

Salaries & Wages Professional Staff	Salaries & Wages Support Staff	Salaries & Wages Student Assistants	Total Salaries & Wages	Other Operating Expend.	Total Library Expend.	
(22)	(23)	(24)	(25)	(26)	(27)	(Survey Question #)
						Institution
1,167,694	650,014	339,543	2,157,251	577,256	4,691,716	Indiana/Purdue, Indianapolis
1,119,417	608,878	203,332	1,931,627	275,503	3,626,808	Indiana State
1,360,347	1,238,766	303,478	2,902,591	865,029	6,459,392	Kansas State
255,923	99,031	60,899	415,853	241,299	927,904	La Sierra
862,602	694,445	192,192	1,749,239	353,392	4,683,245	Lehigh
U/A	U/A	U/A	1,053,173	51,406	1,870,449	Louisiana Tech
1,520,208	1,812,101	373,769	3,706,078	2,083,600	9,801,028	Louisville
2,369,707	1,563,880	567,090	4,500,677	1,139,286	9,871,944	Loyola, Chicago
699,978	804,094	74,422	1,578,494	484,430	4,550,724	Maine, Orono
1,694,892	1,033,063	313,845	3,041,800	241,607	6,532,836	Marquette
596,397	765,993	144,214	1,506,604	366,459	3,565,060	Maryland, Baltimore Ct.
1,080,251	1,456,135	140,845	2,677,231	423,847	5,160,655	Memphis State
1,653,864	1,069,909	422,715	3,146,488	1,314,455	6,800,033	Miami, Ohio
464,145	294,942	47,990	807,077	259,890	2,210,680	Michigan Technological
842,350	522,696	191,229	1,556,275	301,457	3,524,042	Middle Tennessee State
785,701	423,608	211,780	1,421,089	77,199	3,621,062	Mississippi
1,137,703	848,255	361,656	2,347,614	536,540	4,341,153	Missouri, Kansas City
266,987	312,062	39,367	618,416	249,693	1,815,487	Missouri, Rolla
686,553	521,902	170,860	1,379,315	104,457	2,812,150	Missouri, St. Louis
666,951	547,141	50,480	1,264,572	332,306	2,933,461	Montana State
3,208,277	4,528,414	0	7,736,691	1,528,547	13,764,572	Montreal
1,383,063	1,355,682	339,876	3,078,621	552,187	6,134,595	Nevada, Reno
1,391,029	1,855,981	73,597	3,320,608	280,884	4,777,009	New Brunswick
668,288	1,079,895	154,485	1,902,668	263,577	4,508,232	New Hampshire
1,367,060	953,182	300,000	2,620,242	679,752	5,095,178	New Mexico State
706,024	535,444	165,256	1,406,724	142,964	2,713,219	New Orleans
331,174	353,682	32,560	717,416	194,216	1,628,256	New School
958,374	1,135,168	208,712	2,302,254	556,722	4,688,242	North Carolina, Greensboro
U/A	982,123	83,440	1,065,563	390,885	2,507,787	North Dakota State
1,313,902	1,191,913	342,991	2,848,806	731,272	5,305,187	North Texas
1,305,231	886,798	1,286,472	3,478,501	507,491	7,700,739	Northeastern
820,455	1,090,790	300,911	2,212,156	232,200	4,920,135	Northern Arizona
723,406	864,259	71,567	1,659,232	680,442	3,553,508	Northern Colorado
1,885,659	1,767,450	487,171	4,140,280	527,902	8,003,300	Northern Illinois
2,138,845	1,671,739	585,839	4,396,423	2,844,299	10,441,638	Ohio
829,277	857,657	173,452	1,860,386	319,805	3,972,790	Old Dominion
U/A	U/A	U/A	5,116,561	494,054	8,519,716	Ottawa
391,127	417,049	61,654	869,830	137,141	1,729,989	Pacific
675,125	421,984	91,039	1,188,148	590,322	2,601,136	Pepperdine
459,918	130,568	17,848	608,334	280,454	1,305,891	Polytechnic

U/A - Unavailable   N/A - Not Applicable

Lib. No.	Institution	Notes	Monographs (16)	Current Serials (17)	Other Library Materials (18)	Misc. Materials (19)	Total Library Materials (20)	Contract Binding (21)
	(Survey Question #)							
81	Portland State	+	715,012	1,306,670	93,627	160,658	2,275,967	82,000
82	Puerto Rico		773,052	1,474,147	U/A	0	2,247,199	7,000
83	Rhode Island	Bb+	417,201	1,356,590	150,989	0	1,924,780	52,632
84	Rockefeller	b	52,176	396,088	667	104,154	553,085	28,837
85	SUNY, Binghamton	b+	973,425	1,867,083	302,476	91,694	3,234,678	87,394
86	SUNY Coll. Env. Sci. & For.	b+	78,868	372,412	16,675	36,183	504,138	11,437
87	San Diego State	b+	579,447	1,009,985	U/A	0	1,589,432	79,109
88	San Francisco	Bb+	498,978	383,228	134,535	N/A	1,016,741	49,966
89	South Dakota	b+	415,170	455,979	128,775	234,639	1,234,563	25,000
90	South Dakota State	b+	425,829	733,128	88,350	0	1,247,307	27,034
91	South Florida	MB+	1,128,032	2,387,973	709,567	213,483	4,439,055	205,935
92	Southern Methodist	Lb+	1,069,308	1,605,725	143,395	0	2,818,428	96,855
93	Southern Mississippi	b+	167,614	1,075,358	216,742	0	1,459,714	43,557
94	Southwestern Louisiana	b+	245,955	902,788	141,900	0	1,290,643	46,307
95	St. John's	LBb+	597,376	2,053,262	161,991	0	2,812,629	47,314
96	St. Louis	LMB+	782,289	2,022,723	333,056	156,160	3,294,228	94,315
97	Stevens Inst. of Tech.	+	70,000	17,610	108,505	69,000	265,115	14,550
98	Teachers College	b+	53,965	220,780	9,162	1,340	285,247	25,750
99	Tennessee Tech	b+	200,214	684,622	105,857	0	990,693	24,817
100	Texas, Arlington	b+	337,130	968,250	155,297	45,090	1,505,767	75,088
101	Texas, Dallas	B+	344,701	764,715	100,564	203,161	1,413,141	33,074
102	Texas Woman's	Bb+	121,347	311,145	213,948	308,113	954,553	30,000
103	Toledo	Bb+	735,177	1,112,699	14,604	63,558	1,926,038	52,743
104	Tufts	b	614,801	1,117,524	117,269	7,175	1,856,769	79,239
105	Tulsa	Lb+	285,557	1,019,301	143,642	117,993	1,566,493	23,042
106	U.S. International	+	48,082	129,975	4,100	41,641	223,798	0
107	Utah State	+	293,151	1,398,379	173,332	125,406	1,990,268	84,306
108	Vermont	Mb+	1,125,130	1,974,185	260,484	161,926	3,521,725	93,145
109	Virginia Commonwealth	Mb+	1,321,331	2,624,858	617,358	261,396	4,824,943	154,229
110	Wake Forest	LMB+	727,420	2,430,755	388,130	76,544	3,622,849	112,004
111	Wichita State	B+	515,684	781,713	132,841	72,092	1,502,330	41,833
112	William and Mary	LBb+	1,196,014	1,760,014	9,058	0	2,965,086	96,333
113	Windsor	LBb+	414,601	1,099,826	U/A	U/A	1,514,427	52,008
114	Wisconsin, Milwaukee	b+	676,253	1,458,382	164,799	121,098	2,420,532	96,367
115	Wyoming	b+	211,485	1,938,086	20,768	322,874	2,493,213	71,919
116	Yeshiva	LMBb+	377,863	1,373,846	71,592	0	1,823,301	67,248

+ - See Footnotes
L - Includes Law Library
B - Includes Branch Campuses
M - Includes Medical Library
U/A - Unavailable
N/A - Not Applicable

EXPENDITURES

Salaries & Wages Professional Staff	Salaries & Wages Support Staff	Salaries & Wages Student Assistants	Total Salaries & Wages	Other Operating Expend.	Total Library Expend.	
(22)	(23)	(24)	(25)	(26)	(27)	(Survey Question #)
						Institution
1,160,784	1,085,172	222,761	2,468,717	227,915	5,054,599	Portland State
1,407,804	2,763,652	687,489	4,858,945	135,960	7,249,104	Puerto Rico
1,134,829	986,676	207,019	2,328,524	279,534	4,585,470	Rhode Island
200,020	378,412	0	578,432	69,374	1,229,728	Rockefeller
1,427,153	1,859,667	235,136	3,521,956	932,290	7,776,318	SUNY, Binghamton
322,169	96,701	18,046	436,916	12,766	965,257	SUNY Coll. Env. Sci. & For.
1,351,700	1,780,257	535,607	3,667,564	1,725,852	7,061,958	San Diego State
667,682	519,969	76,286	1,263,937	323,474	2,654,118	San Francisco
421,245	292,780	60,129	774,154	173,468	2,207,185	South Dakota
450,186	254,209	84,594	788,989	286,381	2,349,711	South Dakota State
1,963,184	1,611,746	487,188	4,062,118	796,693	9,503,801	South Florida
2,051,075	1,252,352	410,884	3,714,311	1,099,247	7,728,841	Southern Methodist
1,038,738	650,664	225,999	1,915,401	351,677	3,770,349	Southern Mississippi
535,984	538,115	99,452	1,173,551	277,284	2,787,785	Southwestern Louisiana
2,415,036	1,713,911	371,325	4,500,272	3,840,424	11,200,639	St. John's
1,834,566	1,310,845	201,946	3,347,357	595,598	7,331,498	St. Louis
221,125	103,372	102,340	426,837	60,114	766,616	Stevens Inst. of Tech.
1,033,674	350,944	179,178	1,563,796	216,978	2,091,771	Teachers College
516,129	331,290	136,612	984,031	117,585	2,117,126	Tennessee Tech
1,268,628	979,929	122,190	2,370,747	860,222	4,811,824	Texas, Arlington
728,961	642,770	30,867	1,402,598	345,901	3,194,714	Texas, Dallas
501,324	533,133	205,156	1,239,613	71,230	2,295,396	Texas Woman's
1,252,873	1,162,627	297,919	2,713,419	287,983	4,980,183	Toledo
1,000,562	805,020	202,068	2,007,650	372,005	4,315,663	Tufts
821,664	694,727	88,153	1,604,544	170,361	3,364,440	Tulsa
110,574	152,791	17,160	280,525	5,800	510,123	U.S. International
1,305,788	421,841	365,819	2,093,448	675,322	4,843,344	Utah State
1,117,650	1,393,737	167,438	2,678,825	657,002	6,950,697	Vermont
1,365,574	1,700,290	331,291	3,397,155	1,046,286	9,422,613	Virginia Commonwealth
1,434,818	1,313,835	272,127	3,020,780	1,487,088	8,242,721	Wake Forest
783,899	709,012	183,167	1,676,078	497,313	3,717,554	Wichita State
1,347,144	1,104,732	181,410	2,633,286	1,318,624	7,013,329	William and Mary
1,511,943	1,974,816	176,428	3,663,187	170,552	5,400,174	Windsor
1,594,782	1,341,349	450,765	3,386,896	950,551	6,854,346	Wisconsin, Milwaukee
958,834	1,098,392	217,688	2,274,914	308,656	5,148,702	Wyoming
1,340,307	1,080,511	16,616	2,437,434	547,162	4,875,145	Yeshiva

U/A - Unavailable   N/A - Not Applicable

ACRL LIBRARY DATA TABLES 1994-95

SUMMARY DATA: EXPENDITURES

	Monographs	Current Serials	Other Library Materials	Misc. Materials	Total Library Materials	Contract Binding
(Survey Question #)	(16)	(17)	(18)	(19)	(20)	(21)
High	$1,786,248	$3,215,682	$709,567	$1,580,920	$4,824,943	$205,935
Mean	$543,202	$1,150,044	$143,208	$95,351	$1,891,746	$55,589
Median	$453,012	$1,062,668	$94,009	$24,450	$1,770,388	$50,528
Low	$48,082	$17,610	$0	$0	$223,798	$0
Total	$62,468,230	$133,405,078	$13,748,004	$9,821,200	$219,442,512	$6,448,301
Libraries Reporting	115	116	96	103	116	116

ACRL LIBRARY DATA TABLES 1994-95

SUMMARY DATA: EXPENDITURES

Salaries & Wages Professional Staff	Salaries & Wages Support Staff	Salaries & Wages Student Assistants	Total Salaries & Wages	Other Operating Expend.	Total Library Expend.	
(22)	(23)	(24)	(25)	(26)	(27)	(Survey Question #)
$3,208,277	$4,528,414	$1,286,472	$7,736,691	$3,840,424	$13,764,572	High
$1,057,956	$974,290	$222,747	$2,254,162	$578,544	$4,780,040	Mean
$1,041,578	$893,971	$199,120	$2,096,478	$388,504	$4,658,282	Median
$110,574	$33,259	$0	$280,525	$0	$510,123	Low
$118,491,016	$109,120,479	$25,170,386	$261,482,735	$67,111,067	$554,484,617	Total
112	112	113	116	116	116	Libraries Reporting

ACRL LIBRARY DATA TABLES 1994-95

PERSONNEL AND PUBLIC SERVICES

Lib. No.	Institution	Notes	Professional Staff (FTE)	Support Staff (FTE)	Student Assistants (FTE)	Total Staff (FTE)	Library Presentations to Groups	Participants in Group Presentations
	(Survey Question #)		(28)	(29)	(30)	(31)	(32)	(33)
1	Akron	LBb+	39	42	71	152	486	11,368
2	Alabama, Birmingham	MBb+	42	64	46	152	1,211	5,434
3	Alaska	b+	34	44	32	110	423	2,694
4	American	Bb+	21	49	32	102	324	4,983
5	Andrews	b+	12	14	19	45	179	2,505
6	Arkansas, Fayetteville	L+	42	68	44	154	921	5,558
7	Atlanta	b+	23	33	15	71	119	3,150
8	Ball State	b+	40	82	45	167	659	16,648
9	Baylor	LMB+	32	75	43	150	757	17,313
10	Biola	b+	5	8	7	20	104	1,705
11	Bowling Green State	Bb+	51	51	54	156	384	U/A
12	Brandeis	+	30	33	30	93	109	1,813
13	Calgary	LMb+	35	161	19	215	U/A	U/A
14	Calif. Institute of Tech.	B+	14	43	4	61	U/A	U/A
15	Calif., Santa Cruz	b+	27	65	38	130	365	6,868
16	Carnegie-Mellon	b+	33	51	26	110	176	2,160
17	Catholic	b+	30	38	26	94	647	1,700
18	Central Florida	b+	33	53	79	165	328	5,663
19	Claremont	Bb+	18	43	U/A	61	538	U/A
20	Clark	b+	12	15	14	41	234	4,680
21	Clarkson	b	5	8	8	21	33	342
22	Clemson	b+	32	70	22	124	332	5,823
23	Cleveland State	b	21	32	29	82	331	6,173
24	Colorado, Denver	b+	26	62	17	105	398	U/A
25	Colorado School of Mines	+	7	11	8	26	106	1,167
26	Denver	b+	18	40	11	69	265	2,873
27	DePaul	Bb+	28	28	40	96	389	8,051
28	Drake	+	10	15	16	41	41	556
29	Duquesne	b+	15	18	48	81	87	1,174
30	East Texas State	Bb+	16	24	21	61	166	4,000
31	Florida Atlantic	B+	26	50	22	98	162	2,766
32	Fordham	LBb+	36	47	37	120	241	3,618
33	George Mason	LBb+	36	41	29	106	557	6,271
34	George Washington	Bb+	29	107	17	153	268	4,880
35	Georgia State	Lb+	41	91	41	173	354	6,935
36	Hahnemann	Mb+	57	60	52	169	475	3,916
37	Hofstra	L+	36	62	18	116	209	5,063
38	Idaho		23	35	19	77	298	6,501
39	Idaho State	MBb	13	27	21	61	368	4,112
40	Illinois State		38	83	65	186	407	8,793

+ - See Footnotes
L - Includes Law Library
B - Includes Branch Campuses
M - Includes Medical Library
U/A - Unavailable
N/A - Not Applicable

18

ACRL LIBRARY DATA TABLES 1994-95

PERSONNEL AND PUBLIC SERVICES

Reference Transactions	Initial Circulation Transactions	Total Circulation Transactions	Reserve Circulation Transactions	Items Loaned (ILL)	Items Borrowed (ILL)	
(34)	(35)	(36)	(37)	(38)	(39)	(Survey Question #)
						Institution
U/A	215,371	271,506	42,984	36,767	28,141	Akron
238,927	U/A	221,832	73,790	22,797	10,821	Alabama, Birmingham
1,033	100,839	U/A	41,848	10,474	9,204	Alaska
65,024	129,309	200,918	52,374	12,267	8,229	American
26,817	U/A	116,036	U/A	2,893	2,636	Andrews
73,695	U/A	172,583	47,177	11,591	13,940	Arkansas, Fayetteville
41,561	U/A	71,132	17,593	4,915	4,462	Atlanta
89,692	487,074	523,342	118,869	26,180	13,288	Ball State
49,848	U/A	473,619	49,619	15,284	4,904	Baylor
10,500	U/A	97,610	25,973	1,180	889	Biola
38,011	352,376	320,393	111,030	9,658	5,428	Bowling Green State
9,308	U/A	205,733	64,929	7,305	7,499	Brandeis
140,387	756,146	U/A	U/A	14,346	15,050	Calgary
1,500	80,642	U/A	6,352	3,213	10,249	Calif. Institute of Tech.
52,156	U/A	U/A	134,521	7,093	10,786	Calif., Santa Cruz
22,082	U/A	137,569	15,155	5,927	7,558	Carnegie-Mellon
41,577	U/A	142,247	30,581	7,253	4,552	Catholic
62,950	U/A	221,067	110,251	15,771	11,849	Central Florida
30,402	U/A	202,954	45,843	3,357	12,766	Claremont
15,930	39,043	61,818	28,122	7,413	6,667	Clark
3,900	13,621	19,162	42,916	2,704	4,512	Clarkson
65,645	U/A	243,146	32,757	10,326	11,074	Clemson
52,765	160,693	U/A	25,563	11,836	12,062	Cleveland State
75,961	U/A	338,280	51,970	24,505	10,894	Colorado, Denver
6,987	27,444	49,246	42,253	4,289	3,314	Colorado School of Mines
39,634	U/A	234,795	47,671	6,086	6,526	Denver
105,958	105,809	143,459	45,220	52,737	28,946	DePaul
13,492	40,210	57,322	25,886	5,395	4,297	Drake
22,386	49,643	U/A	21,667	1,597	1,176	Duquesne
1,000	U/A	110,224	12,679	13,094	4,846	East Texas State
91,915	U/A	292,136	55,238	12,127	11,561	Florida Atlantic
68,900	U/A	174,683	85,996	8,519	4,962	Fordham
155,648	258,136	258,136	152,084	14,876	12,069	George Mason
260,721	296,929	569,763	69,197	13,272	24,837	George Washington
7,207	310,636	U/A	U/A	14,095	7,647	Georgia State
31,933	U/A	46,273	53,816	11,795	7,847	Hahnemann
75,882	113,414	189,426	24,710	2,921	6,473	Hofstra
48,295	U/A	175,662	53,424	20,256	13,490	Idaho
71,082	442,142	U/A	26,622	8,525	6,378	Idaho State
3,468	257,277	312,646	85,369	48,125	14,176	Illinois State

U/A - Unavailable   N/A - Not Applicable

PERSONNEL AND PUBLIC SERVICES

Lib. No.	Institution	Notes	Professional Staff (FTE)	Support Staff (FTE)	Student Assistants (FTE)	Total Staff (FTE)	Library Presentations to Groups	Participants in Group Presentations
	(Survey Question #)		(28)	(29)	(30)	(31)	(32)	(33)
41	Indiana/Purdue, Indianapolis	B+	35	45	31	111	315	5,207
42	Indiana State	+	29	43	30	102	635	8,786
43	Kansas State	B+	42	63	39	144	117	2,065
44	La Sierra	b	6	8	7	21	40	732
45	Lehigh	b+	19	35	21	75	166	3,752
46	Louisiana Tech	+	15	16	23	54	143	3,133
47	Louisville	LMb+	42	95	46	183	439	7,289
48	Loyola, Chicago	LMBb+	51	79	91	221	989	9,593
49	Maine, Orono	Bb+	23	47	28	98	248	3,637
50	Marquette	L+	41	53	35	129	514	6,743
51	Maryland, Baltimore Ct.	b+	15	39	17	71	137	2,785
52	Memphis State	Bb+	28	79	14	121	356	4,757
53	Miami, Ohio	+	40	52	76	168	604	10,055
54	Michigan Technological	b	16	17	11	44	271	4,093
55	Middle Tennessee State		24	30	24	78	202	U/A
56	Mississippi	B+	24	27	29	80	140	3,074
57	Missouri, Kansas City	LMb+	36	49	35	120	239	4,416
58	Missouri, Rolla	b+	9	16	4	29	74	1,118
59	Missouri, St. Louis	+	23	32	16	71	263	5,972
60	Montana State	b	17	33	6	56	150	2,274
61	Montreal	LMb+	81	218	N/A	299	4,062	13,135
62	Nevada, Reno	MBb+	26	50	47	123	887	16,170
63	New Brunswick	Bb+	24	74	6	104	335	U/A
64	New Hampshire	b+	23	59	37	119	60	1,100
65	New Mexico State	b+	32	55	41	128	389	8,489
66	New Orleans	b+	26	30	18	74	408	2,587
67	New School	b+	11	15	3	29	69	940
68	North Carolina, Greensboro	b+	24	54	27	105	367	U/A
69	North Dakota State	b+	17	28	23	68	108	2,300
70	North Texas	B+	36	68	61	165	337	7,580
71	Northeastern	Bb+	38	42	105	185	577	7,981
72	Northern Arizona		27	53	53	133	459	10,202
73	Northern Colorado	b+	18	33	42	93	554	10,117
74	Northern Illinois	LBb+	45	96	59	200	867	10,518
75	Ohio	MBb+	60	73	74	207	903	19,037
76	Old Dominion	+	23	43	29	95	148	3,302
77	Ottawa	LMBb+	49	144	U/A	193	U/A	8,282
78	Pacific	b+	11	19	17	47	119	1,931
79	Pepperdine	B+	15	18	10	43	76	1,520
80	Polytechnic	B+	12	5	5	22	55	550

+ - See Footnotes   B - Includes Branch Campuses   U/A - Unavailable
L - Includes Law Library   M - Includes Medical Library   N/A - Not Applicable

ACRL LIBRARY DATA TABLES 1994-95

PERSONNEL AND PUBLIC SERVICES

Reference Transactions	Initial Circulation Transactions	Total Circulation Transactions	Reserve Circulation Transactions	Items Loaned (ILL)	Items Borrowed (ILL)	
(34)	(35)	(36)	(37)	(38)	(39)	(Survey Question #)
						Institution
84,948	224,666	U/A	52,965	19,194	13,765	Indiana/Purdue, Indianapolis
120,105	190,638	210,851	28,561	15,678	7,012	Indiana State
U/A	238,466	U/A	39,395	20,019	17,806	Kansas State
3,923	40,396	61,476	U/A	734	275	La Sierra
22,265	U/A	112,100	32,900	7,355	8,789	Lehigh
29,850	U/A	73,934	U/A	2,835	3,878	Louisiana Tech
2,547	260,131	U/A	52,485	10,944	8,454	Louisville
220,775	343,297	374,267	54,017	39,045	17,060	Loyola, Chicago
47,679	165,973	18,339	38,114	42,121	18,456	Maine, Orono
63,596	U/A	214,415	111,623	8,733	9,409	Marquette
48,377	U/A	166,370	136,062	8,211	6,537	Maryland, Baltimore Ct.
381,342	U/A	265,982	U/A	3,752	6,726	Memphis State
141,560	251,557	305,216	136,794	47,838	24,435	Miami, Ohio
25,213	U/A	59,868	43,818	3,150	5,310	Michigan Technological
35,162	U/A	124,746	54,084	4,487	3,119	Middle Tennessee State
3,909	222,313	U/A	22,739	11,049	6,140	Mississippi
115,296	U/A	155,652	32,023	8,688	17,895	Missouri, Kansas City
15,106	U/A	49,232	32,019	6,099	10,653	Missouri, Rolla
75,992	U/A	151,014	56,403	12,011	10,428	Missouri, St. Louis
64,500	106,549	162,141	65,907	13,544	11,111	Montana State
182,559	U/A	710,156	176,089	17,509	7,501	Montreal
154,232	U/A	250,780	77,578	10,557	5,966	Nevada, Reno
81,891	U/A	932,015	U/A	6,088	8,981	New Brunswick
38,870	311,618	343,519	63,516	9,796	8,610	New Hampshire
112,345	U/A	201,657	47,212	11,976	14,921	New Mexico State
101,799	108,410	U/A	53,788	3,263	4,630	New Orleans
32,246	U/A	150,131	42,844	342	210	New School
113,973	218,997	218,997	47,669	7,341	4,592	North Carolina, Greensboro
U/A	150,859	161,886	23,121	12,130	19,714	North Dakota State
364,000	U/A	295,641	47,553	20,335	10,223	North Texas
114,893	U/A	235,683	115,256	16,588	6,185	Northeastern
69,096	152,591	278,929	43,892	16,635	9,033	Northern Arizona
43,652	U/A	222,471	37,245	15,774	7,874	Northern Colorado
155,958	U/A	329,583	161,170	84,711	57,517	Northern Illinois
216,879	U/A	388,350	204,548	18,647	15,768	Ohio
64,116	U/A	241,832	U/A	6,483	5,020	Old Dominion
215,516	U/A	643,815	307,252	20,548	8,145	Ottawa
29,458	U/A	49,745	33,437	5,449	6,027	Pacific
U/A	U/A	45,549	11,911	768	804	Pepperdine
4,320	U/A	34,084	5,490	339	2,189	Polytechnic

U/A - Unavailable   N/A - Not Applicable

PERSONNEL AND PUBLIC SERVICES

Lib. No.	Institution	Notes	Professional Staff (FTE)	Support Staff (FTE)	Student Assistants (FTE)	Total Staff (FTE)	Library Presentations to Groups	Participants in Group Presentations
(Survey Question #)			(28)	(29)	(30)	(31)	(32)	(33)
81	Portland State	+	25	46	28	99	216	4,376
82	Puerto Rico		56	167	82	305	344	6,232
83	Rhode Island	Bb+	19	41	31	91	250	5,803
84	Rockefeller	b	3	9	0	12	110	330
85	SUNY, Binghamton	b+	36	82	41	159	276	3,102
86	SUNY Coll. Env. Sci. & For.	b+	7	6	2	15	21	100
87	San Diego State	b+	31	69	90	190	286	6,422
88	San Francisco	Bb+	13	18	5	36	205	4,116
89	South Dakota	b+	12	18	9	39	160	4,303
90	South Dakota State	b+	14	17	11	42	193	3,358
91	South Florida	MB+	59	108	55	222	599	5,584
92	Southern Methodist	Lb+	56	60	41	157	170	2,928
93	Southern Mississippi	b+	28	39	25	92	237	2,214
94	Southwestern Louisiana	b+	16	31	13	60	232	5,119
95	St. John's	LBb+	36	64	18	118	413	10,637
96	St. Louis	LMB+	57	73	27	157	764	10,176
97	Stevens Inst. of Tech.	+	6	4	10	20	17	333
98	Teachers College	b+	29	15	19	63	255	1,040
99	Tennessee Tech	b+	15	20	17	52	104	2,108
100	Texas, Arlington	b+	37	61	41	139	251	5,352
101	Texas, Dallas	B+	22	37	N/A	59	133	2,238
102	Texas Woman's	Bb+	17	31	26	74	144	2,684
103	Toledo	Bb+	30	42	49	121	296	5,548
104	Tufts	b	25	34	16	75	148	1,171
105	Tulsa	Lb+	25	38	8	71	383	4,720
106	U.S. International	+	5	9	3	17	45	675
107	Utah State	+	41	26	39	106	569	15,948
108	Vermont	Mb+	30	70	28	128	522	6,687
109	Virginia Commonwealth	Mb+	41	89	25	155	758	12,886
110	Wake Forest	LMB+	35	64	30	129	583	7,152
111	Wichita State	B+	23	33	20	76	351	6,123
112	William and Mary	LBb+	33	55	22	110	96	1,677
113	Windsor	LBb+	29	70	17	116	U/A	U/A
114	Wisconsin, Milwaukee	b+	41	53	45	139	512	5,743
115	Wyoming	b+	50	37	24	111	227	3,028
116	Yeshiva	LMBb+	28	47	N/A	75	377	2,701

+ - See Footnotes   B - Includes Branch Campuses   U/A - Unavailable

L - Includes Law Library   M - Includes Medical Library   N/A - Not Applicable

ACRL LIBRARY DATA TABLES 1994-95

PERSONNEL AND PUBLIC SERVICES

Reference Transactions	Initial Circulation Transactions	Total Circulation Transactions	Reserve Circulation Transactions	Items Loaned (ILL)	Items Borrowed (ILL)	
(34)	(35)	(36)	(37)	(38)	(39)	(Survey Question #)
						Institution
4,600	U/A	167,218	57,920	9,460	4,131	Portland State
264,118	U/A	1,028,205	100,864	714	1,766	Puerto Rico
19,787	103,860	139,592	45,135	16,325	12,076	Rhode Island
1,050	3,328	4,760	U/A	2,248	2,173	Rockefeller
40,916	U/A	257,488	91,275	17,973	11,122	SUNY, Binghamton
U/A	U/A	12,217	2,407	3,231	1,373	SUNY Coll. Env. Sci. & For.
336,336	310,606	355,911	62,221	11,925	16,382	San Diego State
26,319	83,402	16,011	1,581	2,052	3,576	San Francisco
18,095	U/A	51,110	27,210	6,641	6,261	South Dakota
19,203	U/A	71,453	33,138	8,977	9,112	South Dakota State
90,282	362,228	405,890	89,750	26,181	15,120	South Florida
133,965	U/A	272,822	U/A	13,263	5,865	Southern Methodist
106,720	U/A	138,124	29,663	4,209	4,884	Southern Mississippi
50,321	U/A	123,353	U/A	5,993	3,103	Southwestern Louisiana
252,558	117,216	122,446	39,529	8,988	3,365	St. John's
40,769	U/A	112,360	43,461	14,733	15,629	St. Louis
3,893	U/A	9,424	1,440	623	5,530	Stevens Inst. of Tech.
84,700	59,060	75,770	15,861	1,289	1,567	Teachers College
18,991	U/A	65,015	36,927	5,286	3,642	Tennessee Tech
126,450	U/A	265,779	49,650	13,555	16,152	Texas, Arlington
650	112,035	U/A	48,093	7,795	8,486	Texas, Dallas
184,704	U/A	117,735	27,699	12,186	13,757	Texas Woman's
50,385	165,855	6,179	172,034	16,517	6,485	Toledo
25,204	173,066	224,809	28,576	4,154	6,899	Tufts
41,316	U/A	86,926	45,860	5,559	8,883	Tulsa
28,056	12,716	18,193	1,247	395	231	U.S. International
29,591	251,205	284,794	106,266	9,059	9,767	Utah State
304,399	187,103	209,302	73,959	12,530	9,484	Vermont
124,408	294,189	321,725	28,385	27,919	9,696	Virginia Commonwealth
68,989	U/A	327,237	41,249	16,063	6,460	Wake Forest
60,937	U/A	255,108	61,751	11,888	11,420	Wichita State
32,195	140,639	153,612	89,280	14,076	6,686	William and Mary
44,058	U/A	685,025	U/A	4,588	6,177	Windsor
2,335	260,979	300,589	132,304	6,726	11,078	Wisconsin, Milwaukee
55,946	236,975	292,459	55,484	22,849	10,794	Wyoming
U/A	158,211	U/A	U/A	8,417	9,439	Yeshiva

U/A - Unavailable   N/A - Not Applicable

ACRL LIBRARY DATA TABLES 1994-95

SUMMARY DATA: PERSONNEL AND PUBLIC SERVICES

	Professional Staff (FTE)	Support Staff (FTE)	Student Assistants (FTE)	Total Staff (FTE)	Library Presentations to Groups	Participants in Group Presentations
(Survey Question #)	(28)	(29)	(30)	(31)	(32)	(33)
High	81	218	105	305	4,062	19,037
Mean	28	49	30	106	362	5,188
Median	27	43	26	102	274	4,376
Low	3	4	0	12	17	100
Total	3,249	5,661	3,342	12,252	40,520	555,092
Libraries Reporting	116	116	111	116	112	107

SUMMARY DATA: PERSONNEL AND PUBLIC SERVICES

Reference Transactions	Initial Circulation Transactions	Total Circulation Transactions	Reserve Circulation Transactions	Items Loaned (ILL)	Items Borrowed (ILL)	
(34)	(35)	(36)	(37)	(38)	(39)	(Survey Question #)
381,342	756,146	1,028,205	307,252	84,711	57,517	High
77,312	193,507	216,572	59,240	12,396	9,274	Mean
50,085	165,973	189,426	47,177	9,727	8,010	Median
650	3,328	4,760	1,247	339	210	Low
8,504,373	10,255,888	21,873,785	6,101,748	1,437,917	1,075,744	Total
110	53	101	103	116	116	Libraries Reporting

ANALYSIS OF SELECTED VARIABLES OF ACRL LIBRARIES

The percentages and ratios below are select indicators that describe the condition of ACRL libraries. The high and low figures indicate the range, while the mean and median indicate the central tendancy of the distributions for ACRL libraries. Note that a distribution is normal when the mean and the median figures are identical. If the mean is larger that the median then the distribution is positively skewed, and if the opposite is true the distribution is negatively skewed.

	Category	High	Mean	Median	Low	Libraries Reporting
1.	Professional Staff as percent of Total Staff	54.55%	27.85%	26.79%	16.28%	116
2.	Support Staff as percent of Total Staff	75.00%	45.27%	43.82%	20.00%	116
3.	Student Assistant Staff as percent of Total Staff	59.26%	26.89%	27.79%	0.00%	116
4.	Ratio of Professional to Support Staff (excluding Student Assistant Staff)	2.40	0.67	0.62	0.22	116
5.	Ratio of Items Loaned to Items Borrowed	3.39	1.36	1.24	0.11	116
6.	Serial Expenditures as percent of Total Library Materials Expenditures	92.38%	60.91%	61.01%	6.64%	116
7.	Total Library Material Expenditures as percent of Total Library Expenditures	65.80%	40.49%	41.15%	13.64%	116
8.	Contract Binding as percent of Total Library Expenditures	3.52%	1.19%	1.15%	0.00%	116
9.	Salary and Wages Expenditures as percent of Total Library Expenditures	74.76%	47.21%	46.38%	32.72%	116
10.	Other Operating Expenditures as percent of Total Library Expenditures	34.29%	11.11%	10.74%	0.00%	116
11.	Unit cost of monographs (per volume)	$126.51	$44.03	$39.27	$13.72	94
12.	Unit cost of serials (per title)	$874.37	$236.57	$221.36	$76.24	73

ACRL LIBRARY DATA TABLES 1994-95

PH.D., FACULTY, AND ENROLLMENT STATISTICS

			Ph.D.s Awarded	Ph.D. Fields	Faculty	ENROLLMENT[†]			
						Total FTE Full-time*	Total Part-time*	Graduate FTE Full-time	Graduate Part-time
	(Survey Question #)		(40)	(41)	(42)	(43)	(44)	(45)	(46)
Lib. No.	Institution	Notes							
1	Akron	LBb+	109	17	729	11,525	9,197	2,276	2,100
2	Alabama, Birmingham	MBb+	97	30	1,746	9,606	5,756	3,016	1,541
3	Alaska	b+	19	12	483	4,381	4,896	492	346
4	American	Bb+	57	15	526	6,661	2,638	1,781	2,128
5	Andrews	b+	30	6	210	2,280	735	686	494
6	Arkansas, Fayetteville	L+	83	23	808	11,670	3,022	1,370	1,385
7	Atlanta	b+	19	7	722	10,778	U/A	1,678	U/A
8	Ball State	b+	20	5	930	16,464	3,926	975	2,376
9	Baylor	LMB+	23	12	599	10,998	1,242	1,176	691
10	Biola	b+	11	1	161	2,473	579	491	441
11	Bowling Green State	Bb+	75	14	696	13,371	2,819	1,533	1,664
12	Brandeis	+	101	21	354	2,817	183	1,115	123
13	Calgary	LMb+	115	35	1,120	17,974	8,329	2,070	816
14	Calif. Institute of Tech.	B+	166	20	363	1,973	N/A	1,050	N/A
15	Calif., Santa Cruz	b+	99	17	383	9,481	636	859	35
16	Carnegie-Mellon	b+	180	54	549	6,308	974	1,968	736
17	Catholic	b+	73	39	379	3,814	2,314	1,635	2,129
18	Central Florida	b+	67	15	604	14,407	10,956	947	2,679
19	Claremont	Bb+	84	14	600	4,675	930	566	826
20	Clark	b+	11	10	165	1,870	692	294	368
21	Clarkson	b	47	8	170	2,187	59	335	20
22	Clemson	b+	96	38	813	13,344	2,946	1,871	2,129
23	Cleveland State	b	30	4	525	7,599	3,742	1,506	3,657
24	Colorado, Denver	b+	18	5	810	16,819	19,524	1,354	3,814
25	Colorado School of Mines	+	43	14	176	2,691	347	484	347
26	Denver	b+	108	U/A	590	5,260	3,232	2,499	2,569
27	DePaul	Bb+	13	3	504	6,459	3,991	2,375	3,064
28	Drake	+	0	U/A	276	3,876	2,078	603	1,433
29	Duquesne	b+	40	5	363	6,269	3,015	1,539	2,073
30	East Texas State	Bb+	8	1	237	4,415	3,337	641	1,979
31	Florida Atlantic	B+	U/A	14	677	6,980	8,505	770	1,588
32	Fordham	LBb+	84	24	500	7,397	7,044	3,104	5,597
33	George Mason	LBb+	70	12	742	11,392	10,382	1,884	6,559
34	George Washington	Bb+	93	30	753	11,016	8,282	5,237	6,856
35	Georgia State	Lb+	126	44	800	11,581	12,149	3,676	3,421
36	Hahnemann	Mb+	20	12	U/A	1,654	595	666	199
37	Hofstra	L+	49	6	455	7,721	3,824	1,326	2,557
38	Idaho		66	24	679	7,398	3,233	1,157	1,890
39	Idaho State	MBb	10	4	489	6,238	2,343	663	1,451
40	Illinois State		27	4	717	16,001	3,589	1,185	1,882

† - Reported data was checked if the number of graduate part-time or full-time students exceeded the respective total number of students.
+ - See Footnotes   B - Includes Branch Campuses   U/A - Unavailable   * - Includes both graduate and
L - Includes Law Library   M - Includes Medical Library   N/A - Not Applicable   undergraduate students

ACRL LIBRARY DATA TABLES 1994-95

PH.D., FACULTY, AND ENROLLMENT STATISTICS

Lib. No.	Institution	Notes	Ph.D.s Awarded	Ph.D. Fields	Faculty	ENROLLMENT† Total FTE Full-time*	Total Part-time*	Graduate FTE Full-time	Graduate Part-time
	(Survey Question #)		(40)	(41)	(42)	(43)	(44)	(45)	(46)
41	Indiana/Purdue, Indianapolis	B+	26	9	U/A	12,051	14,715	2,970	4,313
42	Indiana State	+	26	7	561	8,236	1,717	706	902
43	Kansas State	B+	166	40	894	16,531	4,133	1,810	1,862
44	La Sierra	b	0	U/A	101	1,195	279	49	76
45	Lehigh	b+	125	20	410	4,285	1,308	900	1,141
46	Louisiana Tech	+	0	3	386	7,262	2,685	724	792
47	Louisville	LMb+	61	24	1,763	13,195	8,182	3,451	2,457
48	Loyola, Chicago	LMBb+	98	30	535	7,653	6,153	2,417	3,283
49	Maine, Orono	Bb+	40	22	622	7,944	3,057	1,049	1,268
50	Marquette	L+	59	16	569	8,642	2,124	1,728	1,374
51	Maryland, Baltimore Ct.	b+	42	17	366	6,754	3,561	617	890
52	Memphis State	Bb+	62	12	758	10,454	4,642	2,232	2,530
53	Miami, Ohio	+	43	10	767	14,280	1,601	1,068	804
54	Michigan Technological	b	43	17	400	6,006	454	650	34
55	Middle Tennessee State		0	U/A	689	12,091	3,017	240	1,772
56	Mississippi	B+	152	24	449	8,944	1,493	1,678	766
57	Missouri, Kansas City	LMb+	38	7	546	9,962	4,598	773	2,672
58	Missouri, Rolla	b+	60	18	263	5,317	1,155	487	547
59	Missouri, St. Louis	+	24	9	506	6,428	9,160	1,312	1,540
60	Montana State	b	40	12	460	9,249	1,697	577	585
61	Montreal	LMb+	231	75	1,472	19,176	13,331	6,573	1,365
62	Nevada, Reno	MBb+	60	33	517	7,256	4,490	932	2,079
63	New Brunswick	Bb+	19	15	539	9,672	1,271	803	557
64	New Hampshire	b+	51	21	566	11,268	2,729	917	1,417
65	New Mexico State	b+	66	17	865	12,413	3,230	1,563	983
66	New Orleans	b+	37	10	520	9,164	6,319	1,068	2,721
67	New School	b+	46	6	175	3,648	3,286	922	1,853
68	North Carolina, Greensboro	b+	46	11	570	8,443	4,215	976	1,899
69	North Dakota State	b+	24	19	404	7,800	1,865	328	649
70	North Texas	B+	193	40	1,117	13,913	5,105	2,692	3,895
71	Northeastern	Bb+	75	20	760	13,576	11,510	2,829	2,111
72	Northern Arizona		355	8	667	12,970	6,272	1,420	3,804
73	Northern Colorado	b+	28	9	421	8,969	1,457	914	680
74	Northern Illinois	LBb+	47	9	893	14,487	6,193	1,872	4,257
75	Ohio	MBb+	116	53	921	22,062	5,786	2,557	982
76	Old Dominion	+	79	21	632	10,032	7,045	342	1,816
77	Ottawa	LMBb+	U/A	29	1,217	16,306	7,990	2,174	1,413
78	Pacific	b+	4	2	267	3,596	578	897	328
79	Pepperdine	B+	0	U/A	371	5,890	1,835	3,003	1,419
80	Polytechnic	B+	43	10	176	1,560	1,839	251	1,666

† - Reported data was checked if the number of graduate part-time or full-time students exceeded the respective total number of students.

+ - See Footnotes   B - Includes Branch Campuses   U/A - Unavailable   * - Includes both graduate and

L - Includes Law Library   M - Includes Medical Library   N/A - Not Applicable   undergraduate students

PH.D., FACULTY, AND ENROLLMENT STATISTICS

| | | | Ph.D.s Awarded | Ph.D. Fields | Faculty | ENROLLMENT† | | | |
						Total FTE Full-time*	Total Part-time*	Graduate FTE Full-time	Graduate Part-time
	(Survey Question #)		(40)	(41)	(42)	(43)	(44)	(45)	(46)
Lib. No.	Institution	Notes							
81	Portland State	+	20	6	512	7,570	5,213	1,500	2,643
82	Puerto Rico		30	9	1,064	12,058	2,940	1,374	2,313
83	Rhode Island	Bb+	97	41	672	8,487	2,183	1,151	2,330
84	Rockefeller	b	18	6	219	126	N/A	126	N/A
85	SUNY, Binghamton	b+	104	21	490	9,811	2,278	1,058	1,716
86	SUNY Coll. Env. Sci. & For.	b+	29	5	120	1,339	397	268	328
87	San Diego State	b+	18	9	1,316	19,386	8,401	2,524	3,023
88	San Francisco	Bb+	N/A	N/A	283	6,808	1,599	2,305	1,053
89	South Dakota	b+	48	7	392	6,884	1,868	842	1,013
90	South Dakota State	b+	7	5	471	7,548	2,150	382	1,029
91	South Florida	MB+	104	23	1,785	18,070	17,973	2,905	6,693
92	Southern Methodist	Lb+	47	17	483	6,611	2,403	1,704	2,063
93	Southern Mississippi	b+	80	19	618	8,345	1,111	1,234	897
94	Southwestern Louisiana	b+	31	7	669	12,550	4,239	542	834
95	St. John's	LBb+	13	3	775	13,070	4,750	1,928	3,184
96	St. Louis	LMB+	118	18	491	6,673	7,094	2,059	2,495
97	Stevens Inst. of Tech.	+	22	15	136	U/A	U/A	U/A	U/A
98	Teachers College	b+	35	31	125	2,138	2,421	2,138	2,421
99	Tennessee Tech	b+	8	1	359	6,366	886	96	879
100	Texas, Arlington	b+	84	18	644	12,766	10,607	1,966	2,395
101	Texas, Dallas	B+	U/A	U/A	282	3,312	5,175	1,086	2,674
102	Texas Woman's	Bb+	89	53	454	4,927	4,925	1,190	2,878
103	Toledo	Bb+	71	28	756	14,639	5,215	1,561	1,692
104	Tufts	b	31	17	339	4,550	473	862	450
105	Tulsa	Lb+	23	12	330	3,620	959	373	404
106	U.S. International	+	U/A	U/A	55	1,225	U/A	U/A	U/A
107	Utah State	+	64	50	635	11,945	8,426	866	3,473
108	Vermont	Mb+	53	20	701	8,007	2,223	932	644
109	Virginia Commonwealth	Mb+	109	20	1,564	13,371	8,152	2,198	3,374
110	Wake Forest	LMB+	30	12	912	3,607	921	1,538	755
111	Wichita State	B+	22	8	487	6,437	4,763	826	1,943
112	William and Mary	LBb+	29	6	492	6,790	919	1,464	765
113	Windsor	LBb+	30	9	460	9,693	2,062	1,508	160
114	Wisconsin, Milwaukee	b+	79	17	852	12,366	10,618	1,312	3,428
115	Wyoming	b+	60	26	635	8,763	2,598	921	1,410
116	Yeshiva	LMBb+	53	21	U/A	3,006	558	884	526

† - Reported data was checked if the number of graduate part-time or full-time students exceeded the respective total number of students.

+ - See Footnotes   B - Includes Branch Campuses   U/A - Unavailable   * - Includes both graduate and

L - Includes Law Library   M - Includes Medical Library   N/A - Not Applicable   undergraduate students

ACRL LIBRARY DATA TABLES 1994-95

SUMMARY DATA: PH.D., FACULTY, AND ENROLLMENT STATISTICS

| | Ph.D.s Awarded | Ph.D. Fields | Faculty | ENROLLMENT[†] | | | |
| | | | | Total FTE Full-time* | Total Part-time* | Graduate FTE Full-time | Graduate Part-time |
(Survey Question #)	(40)	(41)	(42)	(43)	(44)	(45)	(46)
High	355	75	1,785	22,062	19,524	6,573	6,856
Mean	60	17	594	8,621	4,240	1,412	1,814
Median	47	15	535	7,944	3,022	1,167	1,588
Low	0	1	55	126	59	49	20
Total	6,668	1,884	67,096	991,367	470,618	160,947	201,350
Libraries Reporting	111	108	113	115	111	114	111

[†] - Reported data was checked if the number of graduate part-time or full-time students exceeded the respective total number of students.
* - Includes both graduate and undergraduate students.

1994-95
RANK ORDER TABLES
OF ACRL LIBRARIES

SUMMARY OF RANK ORDER TABLES FOR ACRL LIBRARIES

The following summary table presents the rank for each ACRL library in each of the eighteen categories for which rank order tables are prepared. The table numbers in the chart below refer to the data categories listed in the summary table. The libraries reporting indicates the number of ACRL libraries supplying data in each category.

Table	Data Category	Libraries Reporting
1	Volumes in Library	115
2	Volumes Added (Gross)	110
3	Current Serials Total	116
4	Microform Units	116
5	Government Documents	95
6	Total Library Materials Expenditures	116
7	Total Salaries and Wages Expenditures	116
8	Other Operating Expenditures	96
9	Total Library Expenditures	116
10	Monographs Purchased	94
11	Monographs Expenditures	115
12	Current Serials Purchased	73
13	Current Serials Expenditures	116
14	Total Items Loaned	116
15	Total Items Borrowed	116
16	Professional Staff (FTE)	116
17	Support Staff (FTE)	116
18	Total Staff (FTE)	116

The quantitative rank order tables are not indicative of performance and outcomes and should not be used as measures of library quality. In comparing any individual library to ACRL medians or to other ACRL members, one must be careful to make such comparisons within the context of differing institutional and local goals and characteristics.

SUMMARY OF RANK ORDER TABLES FOR ACRL LIBRARIES

RANK ORDER TABLES

Lib. No.	Institution	1	2	3	4	5	6	7	8	9	10	11	12	13	14	15	16	17	18
1	Akron	7	U/A	49	36	U/A	27	39	U/A	35	11	15	U/A	32	7	3	24	61	26
2	Alabama, Birmingham	43	12	68	60	78	30	34	45	24	45	49	34	21	13	36	13	27	26
3	Alaska	49	62	52	72	57	92	35	15	39	U/A	U/A	U/A	96	56	48	38	56	50
4	American	75	63	90	81	U/A	82	58	44	67	18	59	U/A	86	42	57	79	49	58
5	Andrews	83	86	93	96	N/A	106	94	U/A	99	65	69	U/A	110	102	105	101	107	98
6	Arkansas, Fayetteville	15	34	5	12	17	17	42	22	31	32	39	4	13	52	19	13	24	24
7	Atlanta	90	82	107	91	N/A	15	76	73	54	40	18	66	93	89	95	71	76	81
8	Ball State	42	36	72	83	73	62	16	17	32	29	54	U/A	72	10	23	22	12	16
9	Baylor	10	U/A	31	65	20	41	36	6	36	U/A	21	U/A	73	30	88	42	16	28
10	Biola	105	102	112	102	N/A	114	114	82	114	86	107	72	112	109	112	113	111	112
11	Bowling Green State	5	4	66	22	39	44	11	81	27	42	22	U/A	50	59	84	8	45	22
12	Brandeis	50	49	56	84	40	43	64	53	60	20	34	43	52	74	64	46	76	66
13	Calgary	U/A	U/A	10	4	U/A	24	4	U/A	12	U/A	41	U/A	14	33	16	35	3	5
14	Calif. Institute of Tech.	89	74	69	95	65	53	69	U/A	64	U/A	94	U/A	27	99	41	97	57	88
15	Calif., Santa Cruz	34	23	37	89	68	31	10	57	8	U/A	20	U/A	36	76	38	58	26	33
16	Carnegie-Mellon	59	61	85	85	78	56	45	25	42	U/A	56	49	49	84	62	39	45	50
17	Catholic	18	38	32	58	78	91	70	67	78	69	70	10	88	75	93	46	69	65
18	Central Florida	69	16	74	35	70	19	46	U/A	34	U/A	1	39	51	28	28	39	40	17
19	Claremont	28	33	57	55	13	42	62	83	59	38	38	26	46	96	24	83	57	88
20	Clark	92	89	100	110	N/A	100	102	68	103	71	91	61	99	71	69	101	103	102
21	Clarkson	108	98	95	107	78	105	115	51	111	U/A	111	58	98	104	94	113	111	110
22	Clemson	62	24	22	68	18	40	50	U/A	37	43	75	17	18	57	34	42	20	38
23	Cleveland State	56	51	82	92	78	69	63	U/A	73	44	85	U/A	44	50	27	79	81	70
24	Colorado, Denver	76	66	79	67	78	78	27	87	44	49	67	U/A	74	11	35	60	31	55
25	Colorado School of Mines	113	104	106	66	38	107	110	94	108	90	109	67	94	92	102	109	108	108
26	Denver	37	50	67	75	12	65	86	58	82	25	31	U/A	77	82	71	83	66	85
27	DePaul	93	59	75	98	U/A	63	60	U/A	65	26	36	42	64	2	2	54	87	63
28	Drake	96	90	91	88	67	103	103	59	106	58	100	55	95	87	96	107	103	102
29	Duquesne	101	100	104	109	U/A	90	106	61	102	83	83	65	106	107	111	92	95	71
30	East Texas State	71	92	105	78	33	108	96	75	104	72	99	U/A	108	40	90	89	92	88
31	Florida Atlantic	74	46	81	2	50	48	71	76	69	70	61	U/A	87	45	29	60	47	61
32	Fordham	8	47	19	25	43	26	32	11	30	30	23	U/A	39	67	87	28	51	42
33	George Mason	72	18	30	30	48	7	48	4	19	5	6	9	20	31	26	28	64	53
34	George Washington	20	39	25	52	78	23	23	96	17	24	24	8	28	38	4	50	6	25
35	Georgia State	27	27	23	24	11	6	20	7	10	8	2	5	25	34	61	17	9	13
36	Hahnemann	110	95	92	116	78	83	91	U/A	86	88	81	U/A	80	51	60	4	34	14
37	Hofstra	39	U/A	94	19	55	55	26	16	40	27	42	U/A	67	101	73	28	31	46
38	Idaho	63	41	24	59	22	74	73	93	76	54	80	30	53	16	22	71	73	74
39	Idaho State	91	85	88	33	32	94	87	72	92	63	84	52	89	66	75	99	89	88
40	Illinois State	23	37	65	29	37	49	19	24	38	33	43	38	59	3	18	25	11	10

U/A - Unavailable   N/A - Not Applicable

33

SUMMARY OF RANK ORDER TABLES FOR ACRL LIBRARIES

RANK ORDER TABLES

Lib. No.	Institution	1	2	3	4	5	6	7	8	9	10	11	12	13	14	15	16	17	18
41	Indiana/Purdue, Indianapolis	102	42	76	71	69	52	57	70	56	U/A	40	45	68	18	20	35	55	48
42	Indiana State	29	22	63	76	78	77	65	36	74	U/A	58	33	82	29	65	50	57	58
43	Kansas State	21	32	40	14	4	25	33	74	29	37	25	19	22	17	9	13	30	29
44	La Sierra	107	106	110	106	78	115	113	U/A	113	84	102	70	114	111	114	111	111	110
45	Lehigh	38	29	48	38	58	28	72	23	58	51	52	31	29	72	53	81	73	76
46	Louisiana Tech	103	97	99	34	14	101	97	78	100	79	105	56	92	103	98	92	101	95
47	Louisville	22	2	15	39	U/A	5	13	14	5	U/A	14	U/A	3	54	56	13	8	12
48	Loyola, Chicago	16	5	17	57	66	4	5	3	4	6	3	U/A	6	6	10	8	14	4
49	Maine, Orono	60	53	54	54	2	33	78	63	62	36	47	22	24	5	7	71	51	61
50	Marquette	41	17	38	77	78	14	30	69	28	15	13	14	15	64	47	17	40	34
51	Maryland, Baltimore Ct.	79	70	80	82	63	64	81	85	77	U/A	60	U/A	48	69	70	92	67	81
52	Memphis State	47	96	29	7	29	46	41	49	45	U/A	73	29	31	95	67	54	14	40
53	Miami, Ohio	9	1	58	10	23	38	28	19	26	14	26	U/A	45	4	5	22	44	15
54	Michigan Technological	66	78	35	101	78	88	100	65	95	87	106	21	63	100	85	89	99	99
55	Middle Tennessee State	81	73	86	63	U/A	66	80	U/A	80	28	29	U/A	75	91	103	67	85	73
56	Mississippi	65	72	18	73	1	45	82	64	75	U/A	44	3	37	53	79	67	89	72
57	Missouri, Kansas City	53	52	41	31	25	75	52	32	66	53	62	U/A	79	65	8	28	49	42
58	Missouri, Rolla	98	93	109	97	71	98	107	27	101	81	82	69	97	80	39	108	101	106
59	Missouri, St. Louis	78	79	34	26	42	80	85	66	85	64	89	50	69	46	40	71	81	81
60	Montana State	84	101	77	53	U/A	79	88	91	84	78	104	47	47	37	32	86	76	94
61	Montreal	2	6	3	49	78	3	1	U/A	1	10	9	U/A	1	21	63	1	1	2
62	Nevada, Reno	55	35	8	5	5	32	29	U/A	33	48	19	20	33	55	81	60	47	39
63	New Brunswick	40	65	73	6	78	87	25	U/A	55	57	76	44	78	81	51	67	17	57
64	New Hampshire	44	57	60	79	3	36	67	U/A	63	55	97	24	9	58	54	71	36	44
65	New Mexico State	52	56	46	74	28	60	44	60	47	52	72	25	43	47	17	42	37	36
66	New Orleans	77	80	59	23	46	89	83	54	88	77	87	53	81	97	91	60	85	79
67	New School	106	99	111	113	U/A	104	105	79	107	67	98	68	115	115	116	105	103	106
68	North Carolina, Greensboro	58	45	64	64	52	58	54	U/A	57	7	30	36	65	73	92	67	39	55
69	North Dakota State	95	71	47	105	54	93	95	80	91	82	96	46	76	44	6	86	87	86
70	North Texas	32	75	39	8	41	61	37	9	43	31	90	U/A	57	15	42	28	24	17
71	Northeastern	64	30	36	28	59	9	18	62	16	9	8	12	8	23	77	25	61	11
72	Northern Arizona	88	58	53	104	35	35	56	5	50	16	16	U/A	70	22	50	58	40	32
73	Northern Colorado	73	69	84	70	34	86	75	48	79	60	77	U/A	91	27	59	83	76	66
74	Northern Illinois	12	26	6	11	6	12	8	12	13	34	46	6	10	1	1	12	7	7
75	Ohio	4	9	2	17	78	16	7	40	3	U/A	5	U/A	26	19	13	2	18	6
76	Old Dominion	85	77	51	100	62	59	68	42	70	U/A	53	U/A	62	79	86	71	57	64
77	Ottawa	14	25	27	51	10	20	2	N/A	9	23	51	U/A	7	14	58	11	4	8
78	Pacific	99	94	98	94	75	102	99	71	105	61	86	59	102	86	80	105	94	97
79	Pepperdine	104	91	89	103	N/A	99	92	77	90	85	103	U/A	100	110	113	92	95	100
80	Polytechnic	109	110	114	111	78	111	108	55	109	94	112	U/A	109	116	106	101	115	109

U/A - Unavailable　　　　　　N/A - Not Applicable

RANK ORDER TABLES

Lib. No.	Institution	1	2	3	4	5	6	7	8	9	10	11	12	13	14	15	16	17	18
81	Portland State	51	54	20	20	30	37	47	50	48	17	35	15	42	60	97	64	54	60
82	Puerto Rico	19	8	50	37	U/A	39	3	U/A	20	56	28	23	34	112	108	6	2	1
83	Rhode Island	45	64	13	48	16	51	53	31	61	73	64	28	41	25	25	81	64	69
84	Rockefeller	112	108	115	115	76	109	109	95	110	93	114	73	103	105	107	116	109	116
85	SUNY, Binghamton	11	10	33	46	36	13	17	13	14	1	17	11	19	20	31	28	12	19
86	SUNY Coll. Env. Sci. & For.	114	105	108	108	78	110	111	86	112	91	108	71	105	98	110	109	114	115
87	San Diego State	36	43	62	1	19	67	14	U/A	21	35	50	35	61	48	11	45	23	9
88	San Francisco	82	68	102	90	53	95	89	37	89	47	57	64	104	106	100	99	95	105
89	South Dakota	97	88	96	93	49	85	104	39	96	68	65	62	101	78	76	101	95	104
90	South Dakota State	94	81	87	87	45	84	101	52	93	46	63	54	85	63	49	97	99	101
91	South Florida	13	11	42	3	24	2	9	1	6	2	10	13	5	9	15	3	5	3
92	Southern Methodist	1	13	55	41	U/A	21	12	34	15	21	12	27	30	39	82	6	34	20
93	Southern Mississippi	57	103	71	18	9	73	66	20	71	76	95	41	58	93	89	54	67	68
94	Southwestern Louisiana	70	76	61	32	61	81	93	35	87	66	88	32	71	83	104	89	83	92
95	St. John's	30	20	7	16	77	22	6	29	2	4	48	1	11	62	101	28	27	45
96	St. Louis	17	21	12	56	47	11	24	10	18	41	27	2	12	32	14	4	18	20
97	Stevens Inst. of Tech.	115	109	116	114	U/A	113	112	43	115	92	110	U/A	116	113	83	111	116	112
98	Teachers College	86	87	103	99	N/A	112	79	89	98	89	113	63	111	108	109	50	103	87
99	Tennessee Tech	100	83	78	61	64	96	98	46	97	U/A	93	48	90	88	99	92	93	96
100	Texas, Arlington	54	28	45	45	U/A	71	51	30	53	75	74	U/A	66	36	12	27	33	30
101	Texas, Dallas	87	40	83	43	U/A	76	84	47	83	U/A	71	U/A	84	70	55	78	71	93
102	Texas Woman's	67	84	96	50	N/A	97	90	21	94	80	101	57	107	43	21	86	83	79
103	Toledo	61	48	70	42	15	50	38	88	49	U/A	32	37	55	24	72	46	61	40
104	Tufts	80	55	101	80	31	54	61	41	68	13	45	60	54	94	66	64	75	76
105	Tulsa	68	67	43	15	27	68	77	33	81	59	79	18	60	85	52	64	69	81
106	U.S. International	111	107	113	112	78	116	116	92	116	U/A	115	U/A	113	114	115	113	109	114
107	Utah State	26	3	11	21	74	47	59	26	52	62	78	40	38	61	43	17	91	53
108	Vermont	31	31	4	47	7	10	40	18	23	U/A	11	U/A	16	41	45	46	20	36
109	Virginia Commonwealth	35	7	28	13	51	1	21	2	7	3	4	16	2	8	44	17	10	23
110	Wake Forest	25	19	9	40	60	8	31	8	11	12	33	U/A	4	26	74	35	27	34
111	Wichita State	48	60	14	69	26	72	74	38	72	39	55	51	83	49	30	71	76	75
112	William and Mary	24	14	21	27	21	18	43	90	22	19	7	7	23	35	68	39	37	50
113	Windsor	3	U/A	1	86	44	70	15	U/A	41	50	66	U/A	56	90	78	50	20	46
114	Wisconsin, Milwaukee	6	15	44	44	56	34	22	28	25	22	37	U/A	35	77	33	17	40	30
115	Wyoming	33	44	16	9	8	29	55	84	46	74	92	U/A	17	12	37	10	71	48
116	Yeshiva	46	U/A	26	62	72	57	49	56	51	U/A	68	U/A	40	68	46	54	51	76

U/A - Unavailable   N/A - Not Applicable

RANK ORDER TABLE 1
VOLUMES IN LIBRARY

Rank	Institution	Value	Rank	Institution	Value
1	Southern Methodist	2,273,228	59	Carnegie-Mellon	873,540
2	Montreal	2,196,734	60	Maine, Orono	873,431
3	Windsor	2,188,943	61	Toledo	868,378
4	Ohio	1,992,066	62	Clemson	860,260
5	Bowling Green State	1,963,805	63	Idaho	847,233
6	Wisconsin, Milwaukee	1,897,378	64	Northeastern	808,509
7	Akron	1,691,709	65	Mississippi	797,387
8	Fordham	1,613,828	66	Michigan Technological	795,312
9	Miami, Ohio	1,563,098	67	Texas Woman's	794,455
10	Baylor	1,560,980	68	Tulsa	790,276
11	SUNY, Binghamton	1,544,905	69	Central Florida	781,669
12	Northern Illinois	1,525,438	70	Southwestern Louisiana	717,776
13	South Florida	1,524,685	71	East Texas State	700,251
14	Ottawa	1,479,046	72	George Mason	671,528
15	Arkansas, Fayetteville	1,452,137	73	Northern Colorado	645,121
16	Loyola, Chicago	1,407,134	74	Florida Atlantic	638,071
17	St. Louis	1,403,861	75	American	635,767
18	Catholic	1,368,049	76	Colorado, Denver	624,500
19	Puerto Rico	1,367,167	77	New Orleans	614,985
20	George Washington	1,352,922	78	Missouri, St. Louis	612,621
21	Kansas State	1,340,443	79	Maryland, Baltimore Ct.	610,164
22	Louisville	1,315,284	80	Tufts	607,816
23	Illinois State	1,279,887	81	Middle Tennessee State	604,017
24	William and Mary	1,277,308	82	San Francisco	603,341
25	Wake Forest	1,276,536	83	Andrews	601,623
26	Utah State	1,261,463	84	Montana State	574,602
27	Georgia State	1,245,668	85	Old Dominion	557,561
28	Claremont	1,213,831	86	Teachers College	557,404
29	Indiana State	1,209,617	87	Texas, Dallas	554,547
30	St. John's	1,202,376	88	Northern Arizona	550,014
31	Vermont	1,153,752	89	Calif. Institute of Tech.	536,913
32	North Texas	1,153,273	90	Atlanta	529,833
33	Wyoming	1,134,211	91	Idaho State	522,064
34	Calif., Santa Cruz	1,132,156	92	Clark	520,943
35	Virginia Commonwealth	1,130,562	93	DePaul	502,495
36	San Diego State	1,121,934	94	South Dakota State	501,767
37	Denver	1,107,670	95	North Dakota State	483,458
38	Lehigh	1,105,636	96	Drake	475,912
39	Hofstra	1,099,900	97	South Dakota	460,749
40	New Brunswick	1,085,567	98	Missouri, Rolla	455,302
41	Marquette	1,074,199	99	Pacific	440,148
42	Ball State	1,067,498	100	Tennessee Tech	400,565
43	Alabama, Birmingham	1,064,930	101	Duquesne	378,724
44	New Hampshire	1,059,055	102	Indiana/Purdue, Indianapolis	363,285
45	Rhode Island	1,057,197	103	Louisiana Tech	359,895
46	Yeshiva	1,013,674	104	Pepperdine	339,460
47	Memphis State	1,010,046	105	Biola	249,673
48	Wichita State	993,724	106	New School	247,943
49	Alaska	992,427	107	La Sierra	225,311
50	Brandeis	981,911	108	Clarkson	224,306
51	Portland State	981,391	109	Polytechnic	197,300
52	New Mexico State	973,265	110	Hahnemann	197,153
53	Missouri, Kansas City	962,529	111	U.S. International	196,934
54	Texas, Arlington	957,936	112	Rockefeller	182,249
55	Nevada, Reno	911,567	113	Colorado School of Mines	140,518
56	Cleveland State	901,022	114	SUNY Coll. Env. Sci. & For.	115,488
57	Southern Mississippi	877,109	115	Stevens Inst. of Tech.	106,288
58	North Carolina, Greensboro	876,640	116	Calgary	U/A

U/A - Unavailable   Figures for some institutions include government documents (see also Rank Order Table 5)

RANK ORDER TABLE 2
VOLUMES ADDED (GROSS)

Rank	Institution	Value	Rank	Institution	Value
1	Miami, Ohio	98,615	59	DePaul	22,939
2	Louisville	84,721	60	Wichita State	22,576
3	Utah State	74,606	61	Carnegie-Mellon	22,305
4	Bowling Green State	63,562	62	Alaska	21,179
5	Loyola, Chicago	62,956	63	American	20,549
6	Montreal	60,972	64	Rhode Island	19,368
7	Virginia Commonwealth	53,218	65	New Brunswick	19,106
8	Puerto Rico	51,195	66	Colorado, Denver	19,052
9	Ohio	49,552	67	Tulsa	18,453
10	SUNY, Binghamton	48,037	68	San Francisco	18,248
11	South Florida	46,646	69	Northern Colorado	18,034
12	Alabama, Birmingham	46,551	70	Maryland, Baltimore Ct.	17,735
13	Southern Methodist	46,270	71	North Dakota State	17,641
14	William and Mary	44,271	72	Mississippi	17,609
15	Wisconsin, Milwaukee	41,515	73	Middle Tennessee State	17,170
16	Central Florida	41,114	74	Calif. Institute of Tech.	16,673
17	Marquette	41,000	75	North Texas	16,650
18	George Mason	40,582	76	Southwestern Louisiana	16,542
19	Wake Forest	40,238	77	Old Dominion	15,549
20	St. John's	38,977	78	Michigan Technological	15,091
21	St. Louis	38,503	79	Missouri, St. Louis	14,520
22	Indiana State	37,226	80	New Orleans	14,413
23	Calif., Santa Cruz	36,573	81	South Dakota State	14,116
24	Clemson	36,177	82	Atlanta	13,816
25	Ottawa	35,787	83	Tennessee Tech	12,891
26	Northern Illinois	35,167	84	Texas Woman's	12,177
27	Georgia State	35,158	85	Idaho State	11,866
28	Texas, Arlington	34,831	86	Andrews	11,482
29	Lehigh	34,768	87	Teachers College	10,555
30	Northeastern	33,549	88	South Dakota	10,133
31	Vermont	32,960	89	Clark	9,266
32	Kansas State	32,784	90	Drake	9,072
33	Claremont	31,739	91	Pepperdine	8,529
34	Arkansas, Fayetteville	31,696	92	East Texas State	8,438
35	Nevada, Reno	31,045	93	Missouri, Rolla	8,144
36	Ball State	30,800	94	Pacific	8,070
37	Illinois State	30,584	95	Hahnemann	7,968
38	Catholic	30,346	96	Memphis State	7,868
39	George Washington	30,180	97	Louisiana Tech	6,875
40	Texas, Dallas	29,978	98	Clarkson	6,639
41	Idaho	29,974	99	New School	6,552
42	Indiana/Purdue, Indianapolis	29,943	100	Duquesne	6,476
43	San Diego State	29,415	101	Montana State	6,122
44	Wyoming	29,072	102	Biola	5,891
45	North Carolina, Greensboro	28,638	103	Southern Mississippi	5,098
46	Florida Atlantic	28,187	104	Colorado School of Mines	3,785
47	Fordham	27,761	105	SUNY Coll. Env. Sci. & For.	3,384
48	Toledo	26,886	106	La Sierra	2,993
49	Brandeis	26,695	107	U.S. International	2,900
50	Denver	26,672	108	Rockefeller	2,631
51	Cleveland State	26,504	109	Stevens Inst. of Tech.	1,804
52	Missouri, Kansas City	25,178	110	Polytechnic	609
53	Maine, Orono	24,767	111	Akron	U/A
54	Portland State	24,251	111	Baylor	U/A
55	Tufts	24,038	111	Calgary	U/A
56	New Mexico State	23,860	111	Hofstra	U/A
57	New Hampshire	23,826	111	Windsor	U/A
58	Northern Arizona	23,627	111	Yeshiva	U/A

U/A - Unavailable

RANK ORDER TABLE 3
CURRENT SERIALS TOTAL

Rank	Institution	Value	Rank	Institution	Value
1	Windsor	493,886	59	New Orleans	5,955
2	Ohio	25,564	60	New Hampshire	5,901
3	Montreal	19,270	61	Southwestern Louisiana	5,887
4	Vermont	17,136	62	San Diego State	5,690
5	Arkansas, Fayetteville	16,298	63	Indiana State	5,507
6	Northern Illinois	15,796	64	North Carolina, Greensboro	5,429
7	St. John's	15,171	65	Illinois State	5,402
8	Nevada, Reno	15,091	66	Bowling Green State	5,343
9	Wake Forest	14,891	67	Denver	5,330
10	Calgary	14,478	68	Alabama, Birmingham	5,287
11	Utah State	14,010	69	Calif. Institute of Tech.	5,119
12	St. Louis	13,834	70	Toledo	5,047
13	Rhode Island	13,816	71	Southern Mississippi	4,980
14	Wichita State	13,252	72	Ball State	4,956
15	Louisville	12,812	73	New Brunswick	4,912
16	Wyoming	12,150	74	Central Florida	4,671
17	Loyola, Chicago	11,789	75	DePaul	4,660
18	Mississippi	11,786	76	Indiana/Purdue, Indianapolis	4,508
19	Fordham	11,307	77	Montana State	4,487
20	Portland State	11,299	78	Tennessee Tech	4,182
21	William and Mary	11,213	79	Colorado, Denver	4,177
22	Clemson	11,145	80	Maryland, Baltimore Ct.	4,067
23	Georgia State	11,098	81	Florida Atlantic	4,056
24	Idaho	10,951	82	Cleveland State	3,863
25	George Washington	10,509	83	Texas, Dallas	3,811
26	Yeshiva	10,176	84	Northern Colorado	3,710
27	Ottawa	9,861	85	Carnegie-Mellon	3,561
28	Virginia Commonwealth	9,786	86	Middle Tennessee State	3,507
29	Memphis State	9,701	87	South Dakota State	3,497
30	George Mason	9,533	88	Idaho State	3,302
31	Baylor	9,424	89	Pepperdine	3,186
32	Catholic	9,423	90	American	3,091
33	SUNY, Binghamton	9,300	91	Drake	2,955
34	Missouri, St. Louis	9,163	92	Hahnemann	2,912
35	Michigan Technological	9,155	93	Andrews	2,828
36	Northeastern	8,963	94	Hofstra	2,786
37	Calif., Santa Cruz	8,948	95	Clarkson	2,711
38	Marquette	8,902	96	South Dakota	2,697
39	North Texas	8,858	96	Texas Woman's	2,697
40	Kansas State	8,850	98	Pacific	2,680
41	Missouri, Kansas City	8,793	99	Louisiana Tech	2,635
42	South Florida	8,757	100	Clark	2,633
43	Tulsa	8,283	101	Tufts	2,584
44	Wisconsin, Milwaukee	7,950	102	San Francisco	2,381
45	Texas, Arlington	7,908	103	Teachers College	2,216
46	New Mexico State	7,328	104	Duquesne	2,016
47	North Dakota State	7,182	105	East Texas State	1,975
48	Lehigh	7,140	106	Colorado School of Mines	1,897
49	Akron	6,962	107	Atlanta	1,789
50	Puerto Rico	6,914	108	SUNY Coll. Env. Sci. & For.	1,784
51	Old Dominion	6,905	109	Missouri, Rolla	1,456
52	Alaska	6,889	110	La Sierra	1,422
53	Northern Arizona	6,649	111	New School	1,230
54	Maine, Orono	6,400	112	Biola	1,097
55	Southern Methodist	6,220	113	U.S. International	971
56	Brandeis	6,060	114	Polytechnic	821
57	Claremont	6,029	115	Rockefeller	464
58	Miami, Ohio	6,014	116	Stevens Inst. of Tech.	140

RANK ORDER TABLE 4
MICROFORM UNITS

Rank	Institution	Value	Rank	Institution	Value
1	San Diego State	3,738,123	59	Idaho	1,176,725
2	Florida Atlantic	3,279,194	60	Alabama, Birmingham	1,156,575
3	South Florida	3,194,132	61	Tennessee Tech	1,127,711
4	Calgary	3,134,056	62	Yeshiva	1,117,676
5	Nevada, Reno	2,975,375	63	Middle Tennessee State	1,116,512
6	New Brunswick	2,955,623	64	North Carolina, Greensboro	1,110,219
7	Memphis State	2,871,546	65	Baylor	1,091,804
8	North Texas	2,828,456	66	Colorado School of Mines	1,082,566
9	Wyoming	2,720,746	67	Colorado, Denver	1,079,112
10	Miami, Ohio	2,662,636	68	Clemson	1,075,981
11	Northern Illinois	2,660,060	69	Wichita State	1,024,262
12	Arkansas, Fayetteville	2,649,581	70	Northern Colorado	1,012,488
13	Virginia Commonwealth	2,452,650	71	Indiana/Purdue, Indianapolis	1,008,114
14	Kansas State	2,431,669	72	Alaska	992,228
15	Tulsa	2,416,604	73	Mississippi	983,561
16	St. John's	2,401,059	74	New Mexico State	956,989
17	Ohio	2,321,171	75	Denver	912,115
18	Southern Mississippi	2,265,196	76	Indiana State	889,864
19	Hofstra	2,167,850	77	Marquette	889,055
20	Portland State	2,136,893	78	East Texas State	866,551
21	Utah State	2,134,223	79	New Hampshire	866,478
22	Bowling Green State	2,070,934	80	Tufts	862,224
23	New Orleans	2,069,860	81	American	858,300
24	Georgia State	2,027,368	82	Maryland, Baltimore Ct.	854,735
25	Fordham	2,010,409	83	Ball State	836,556
26	Missouri, St. Louis	1,908,246	84	Brandeis	834,668
27	William and Mary	1,882,891	85	Carnegie-Mellon	809,527
28	Northeastern	1,879,678	86	Windsor	775,828
29	Illinois State	1,865,148	87	South Dakota State	744,653
30	George Mason	1,864,737	88	Drake	710,000
31	Missouri, Kansas City	1,813,413	89	Calif., Santa Cruz	709,462
32	Southwestern Louisiana	1,745,804	90	San Francisco	653,769
33	Idaho State	1,736,824	91	Atlanta	641,724
34	Louisiana Tech	1,734,961	92	Cleveland State	638,325
35	Central Florida	1,713,464	93	South Dakota	569,698
36	Akron	1,686,820	94	Pacific	556,534
37	Puerto Rico	1,665,365	95	Calif. Institute of Tech.	536,907
38	Lehigh	1,658,580	96	Andrews	530,750
39	Louisville	1,621,550	97	Missouri, Rolla	509,889
40	Wake Forest	1,602,327	98	DePaul	501,313
41	Southern Methodist	1,562,468	99	Teachers College	483,631
42	Toledo	1,530,334	100	Old Dominion	450,605
43	Texas, Dallas	1,524,008	101	Michigan Technological	440,508
44	Wisconsin, Milwaukee	1,495,169	102	Biola	407,022
45	Texas, Arlington	1,478,656	103	Pepperdine	399,575
46	SUNY, Binghamton	1,471,103	104	Northern Arizona	369,727
47	Vermont	1,470,155	105	North Dakota State	345,759
48	Rhode Island	1,448,733	106	La Sierra	315,417
49	Montreal	1,390,557	107	Clarkson	269,289
50	Texas Woman's	1,387,220	108	SUNY Coll. Env. Sci. & For.	153,748
51	Ottawa	1,368,610	109	Duquesne	68,208
52	George Washington	1,342,696	110	Clark	60,000
53	Montana State	1,333,061	111	Polytechnic	56,628
54	Maine, Orono	1,327,178	112	U.S. International	41,131
55	Claremont	1,278,959	113	New School	20,703
56	St. Louis	1,276,539	114	Stevens Inst. of Tech.	12,400
57	Loyola, Chicago	1,246,450	115	Rockefeller	20
58	Catholic	1,237,338	116	Hahnemann	3

RANK ORDER TABLE 5
GOVERNMENT DOCUMENTS

Rank	Institution	Value	Rank	Institution	Value
1	Mississippi	2,090,997	59	Northeastern	172,091
2	Maine, Orono	1,942,950	60	Wake Forest	161,990
3	New Hampshire	1,459,576	61	Southwestern Louisiana	160,881
4	Kansas State	1,340,858	62	Old Dominion	159,480
5	Nevada, Reno	1,284,632	63	Maryland, Baltimore Ct.	148,225
6	Northern Illinois	1,227,826	64	Tennessee Tech	136,004
7	Vermont	1,047,513	65	Calif. Institute of Tech.	109,245
8	Wyoming	969,334	66	Loyola, Chicago	91,753
9	Southern Mississippi	966,727	67	Drake	89,758
10	Ottawa	774,352	68	Calif., Santa Cruz	82,608
11	Georgia State	745,932	69	Indiana/Purdue, Indianapolis	80,404
12	Denver	744,077	70	Central Florida	66,800
13	Claremont	717,830	71	Missouri, Rolla	66,051
14	Louisiana Tech	706,818	72	Yeshiva	26,048
15	Toledo	704,138	73	Ball State	10,031
16	Rhode Island	677,374	74	Utah State	5,407
17	Arkansas, Fayetteville	627,514	75	Pacific	3,500
18	Clemson	599,083	76	Rockefeller	1,589
19	San Diego State	592,474	77	St. John's	1,000
20	Baylor	570,556	78	Alabama, Birmingham	0
21	William and Mary	552,595	78	Carnegie-Mellon	0
22	Idaho	550,238	78	Catholic	0
23	Miami, Ohio	535,060	78	Clarkson	0
24	South Florida	533,729	78	Cleveland State	0
25	Missouri, Kansas City	502,969	78	Colorado, Denver	0
26	Wichita State	502,216	78	George Washington	0
27	Tulsa	479,067	78	Hahnemann	0
28	New Mexico State	471,062	78	Indiana State	0
29	Memphis State	458,345	78	La Sierra	0
30	Portland State	455,751	78	Marquette	0
31	Tufts	452,631	78	Michigan Technological	0
32	Idaho State	422,640	78	Montreal	0
33	East Texas State	414,469	78	New Brunswick	0
34	Northern Colorado	411,435	78	Ohio	0
35	Northern Arizona	395,058	78	Polytechnic	0
36	SUNY, Binghamton	381,463	78	SUNY Coll. Env. Sci. & For.	0
37	Illinois State	380,854	78	U.S. International	0
38	Colorado School of Mines	377,910	96	Akron	U/A
39	Bowling Green State	374,520	96	American	U/A
40	Brandeis	371,255	96	Calgary	U/A
41	North Texas	369,562	96	DePaul	U/A
42	Missouri, St. Louis	361,663	96	Duquesne	U/A
43	Fordham	355,480	96	Louisville	U/A
44	Windsor	350,000	96	Middle Tennessee State	U/A
45	South Dakota State	344,212	96	Montana State	U/A
46	New Orleans	321,878	96	New School	U/A
47	St. Louis	308,621	96	Puerto Rico	U/A
48	George Mason	280,234	96	Southern Methodist	U/A
49	South Dakota	275,275	96	Stevens Inst. of Tech.	U/A
50	Florida Atlantic	271,212	96	Texas, Arlington	U/A
51	Virginia Commonwealth	264,611	96	Texas, Dallas	U/A
52	North Carolina, Greensboro	258,406	110	Andrews	N/A
53	San Francisco	243,474	110	Atlanta	N/A
54	North Dakota State	243,046	110	Biola	N/A
55	Hofstra	229,925	110	Clark	N/A
56	Wisconsin, Milwaukee	219,282	110	Pepperdine	N/A
57	Alaska	197,631	110	Teachers College	N/A
58	Lehigh	177,289	110	Texas Woman's	N/A

U/A - Unavailable   N/A - Not Applicable

RANK ORDER TABLE 6
TOTAL LIBRARY MATERIALS EXPENDITURES

Rank	Institution	Value	Rank	Institution	Value
1	Virginia Commonwealth	4,824,943	59	Old Dominion	1,741,510
2	South Florida	4,439,055	60	New Mexico State	1,710,184
3	Montreal	4,386,256	61	North Texas	1,681,507
4	Loyola, Chicago	4,119,446	62	Ball State	1,681,148
5	Louisville	3,924,308	63	DePaul	1,670,607
6	Georgia State	3,838,737	64	Maryland, Baltimore Ct.	1,652,175
7	George Mason	3,656,764	65	Denver	1,632,795
8	Wake Forest	3,622,849	66	Middle Tennessee State	1,626,172
9	Northeastern	3,558,371	67	San Diego State	1,589,432
10	Vermont	3,521,725	68	Tulsa	1,566,493
11	St. Louis	3,294,228	69	Cleveland State	1,545,870
12	Northern Illinois	3,260,283	70	Windsor	1,514,427
13	SUNY, Binghamton	3,234,678	71	Texas, Arlington	1,505,767
14	Marquette	3,182,465	72	Wichita State	1,502,330
15	Atlanta	3,161,840	73	Southern Mississippi	1,459,714
16	Ohio	3,114,421	74	Idaho	1,434,027
17	Arkansas, Fayetteville	3,084,282	75	Missouri, Kansas City	1,414,206
18	William and Mary	2,965,086	76	Texas, Dallas	1,413,141
19	Central Florida	2,928,435	77	Indiana State	1,372,380
20	Ottawa	2,833,706	78	Colorado, Denver	1,309,936
21	Southern Methodist	2,818,428	79	Montana State	1,309,506
22	St. John's	2,812,629	80	Missouri, St. Louis	1,299,667
23	George Washington	2,687,483	81	Southwestern Louisiana	1,290,643
24	Calgary	2,654,827	82	American	1,287,025
25	Kansas State	2,607,772	83	Hahnemann	1,274,777
26	Fordham	2,533,827	84	South Dakota State	1,247,307
27	Akron	2,533,678	85	South Dakota	1,234,563
28	Lehigh	2,524,854	86	Northern Colorado	1,191,775
29	Wyoming	2,493,213	87	New Brunswick	1,139,337
30	Alabama, Birmingham	2,475,732	88	Michigan Technological	1,132,945
31	Calif., Santa Cruz	2,465,676	89	New Orleans	1,123,288
32	Nevada, Reno	2,443,273	90	Duquesne	1,113,846
33	Maine, Orono	2,421,300	91	Catholic	1,103,276
34	Wisconsin, Milwaukee	2,420,532	92	Alaska	1,046,096
35	Northern Arizona	2,379,993	93	North Dakota State	1,036,866
36	New Hampshire	2,309,060	94	Idaho State	1,032,849
37	Portland State	2,275,967	95	San Francisco	1,016,741
38	Miami, Ohio	2,260,574	96	Tennessee Tech	990,693
39	Puerto Rico	2,247,199	97	Texas Woman's	954,553
40	Clemson	2,234,656	98	Missouri, Rolla	926,543
41	Baylor	2,222,873	99	Pepperdine	799,478
42	Claremont	2,216,931	100	Clark	733,291
43	Brandeis	2,135,522	101	Louisiana Tech	730,370
44	Bowling Green State	2,102,203	102	Pacific	713,018
45	Mississippi	2,087,068	103	Drake	705,287
46	Memphis State	2,013,789	104	New School	691,179
47	Utah State	1,990,268	105	Clarkson	645,631
48	Florida Atlantic	1,981,068	106	Andrews	640,110
49	Illinois State	1,926,264	107	Colorado School of Mines	608,496
50	Toledo	1,926,038	108	East Texas State	599,630
51	Rhode Island	1,924,780	109	Rockefeller	553,085
52	Indiana/Purdue, Indianapolis	1,897,305	110	SUNY Coll. Env. Sci. & For.	504,138
53	Calif. Institute of Tech.	1,878,460	111	Polytechnic	417,103
54	Tufts	1,856,769	112	Teachers College	285,247
55	Hofstra	1,856,154	113	Stevens Inst. of Tech.	265,115
56	Carnegie-Mellon	1,852,744	114	Biola	260,425
57	Yeshiva	1,823,301	115	La Sierra	247,640
58	North Carolina, Greensboro	1,799,266	116	U.S. International	223,798

RANK ORDER TABLE 7
TOTAL SALARIES AND WAGES EXPENDITURES

Rank	Institution	Value	Rank	Institution	Value
1	Montreal	7,736,691	59	Utah State	2,093,448
2	Ottawa	5,116,561	60	DePaul	2,060,582
3	Puerto Rico	4,858,945	61	Tufts	2,007,650
4	Calgary	4,778,492	62	Claremont	1,993,587
5	Loyola, Chicago	4,500,677	63	Cleveland State	1,972,827
6	St. John's	4,500,272	64	Brandeis	1,965,923
7	Ohio	4,396,423	65	Indiana State	1,931,627
8	Northern Illinois	4,140,280	66	Southern Mississippi	1,915,401
9	South Florida	4,062,118	67	New Hampshire	1,902,668
10	Calif., Santa Cruz	3,929,317	68	Old Dominion	1,860,386
11	Bowling Green State	3,720,879	69	Calif. Institute of Tech.	1,778,662
12	Southern Methodist	3,714,311	70	Catholic	1,778,025
13	Louisville	3,706,078	71	Florida Atlantic	1,749,750
14	San Diego State	3,667,564	72	Lehigh	1,749,239
15	Windsor	3,663,187	73	Idaho	1,678,507
16	Ball State	3,587,230	74	Wichita State	1,676,078
17	SUNY, Binghamton	3,521,956	75	Northern Colorado	1,659,232
18	Northeastern	3,478,501	76	Atlanta	1,643,414
19	Illinois State	3,465,728	77	Tulsa	1,604,544
20	Georgia State	3,437,872	78	Maine, Orono	1,578,494
21	Virginia Commonwealth	3,397,155	79	Teachers College	1,563,796
22	Wisconsin, Milwaukee	3,386,896	80	Middle Tennessee State	1,556,275
23	George Washington	3,351,109	81	Maryland, Baltimore Ct.	1,506,604
24	St. Louis	3,347,357	82	Mississippi	1,421,089
25	New Brunswick	3,320,608	83	New Orleans	1,406,724
26	Hofstra	3,319,945	84	Texas, Dallas	1,402,598
27	Colorado, Denver	3,285,840	85	Missouri, St. Louis	1,379,315
28	Miami, Ohio	3,146,488	86	Denver	1,295,337
29	Nevada, Reno	3,078,621	87	Idaho State	1,286,244
30	Marquette	3,041,800	88	Montana State	1,264,572
31	Wake Forest	3,020,780	89	San Francisco	1,263,937
32	Fordham	3,004,570	90	Texas Woman's	1,239,613
33	Kansas State	2,902,591	91	Hahnemann	1,221,515
34	Alabama, Birmingham	2,890,774	92	Pepperdine	1,188,148
35	Alaska	2,866,844	93	Southwestern Louisiana	1,173,551
36	Baylor	2,855,933	94	Andrews	1,078,210
37	North Texas	2,848,806	95	North Dakota State	1,065,563
38	Toledo	2,713,419	96	East Texas State	1,056,270
39	Akron	2,697,180	97	Louisiana Tech	1,053,173
40	Vermont	2,678,825	98	Tennessee Tech	984,031
41	Memphis State	2,677,231	99	Pacific	869,830
42	Arkansas, Fayetteville	2,634,950	100	Michigan Technological	807,077
43	William and Mary	2,633,286	101	South Dakota State	788,989
44	New Mexico State	2,620,242	102	Clark	788,095
45	Carnegie-Mellon	2,531,196	103	Drake	779,907
46	Central Florida	2,520,120	104	South Dakota	774,154
47	Portland State	2,468,717	105	New School	717,416
48	George Mason	2,444,020	106	Duquesne	620,521
49	Yeshiva	2,437,434	107	Missouri, Rolla	618,416
50	Clemson	2,387,768	108	Polytechnic	608,334
51	Texas, Arlington	2,370,747	109	Rockefeller	578,432
52	Missouri, Kansas City	2,347,614	110	Colorado School of Mines	578,245
53	Rhode Island	2,328,524	111	SUNY Coll. Env. Sci. & For.	436,916
54	North Carolina, Greensboro	2,302,254	112	Stevens Inst. of Tech.	426,837
55	Wyoming	2,274,914	113	La Sierra	415,853
56	Northern Arizona	2,212,156	114	Biola	411,477
57	Indiana/Purdue, Indianapolis	2,157,251	115	Clarkson	388,549
58	American	2,099,507	116	U.S. International	280,525

RANK ORDER TABLE 8
OTHER OPERATING EXPENDITURES

Rank	Institution	Value	Rank	Institution	Value
1	South Florida	709,567	59	Drake	66,481
2	Virginia Commonwealth	617,358	60	New Mexico State	65,181
3	Loyola, Chicago	574,363	61	Duquesne	63,252
4	George Mason	562,992	62	Northeastern	61,746
5	Northern Arizona	483,106	63	Maine, Orono	61,300
6	Baylor	434,054	64	Mississippi	57,521
7	Georgia State	388,243	65	Michigan Technological	56,240
8	Wake Forest	388,130	66	Missouri, St. Louis	51,474
9	North Texas	338,300	67	Catholic	48,000
10	St. Louis	333,056	68	Clark	47,616
11	Fordham	325,585	69	Marquette	42,667
12	Northern Illinois	322,869	70	Indiana/Purdue, Indianapolis	42,025
13	SUNY, Binghamton	302,476	71	Pacific	40,934
14	Louisville	301,032	72	Idaho State	40,732
15	Alaska	295,089	73	Atlanta	38,193
16	Hofstra	275,572	74	Kansas State	36,126
17	Ball State	267,562	75	East Texas State	35,325
18	Vermont	260,484	76	Florida Atlantic	34,807
19	Miami, Ohio	257,339	77	Pepperdine	34,765
20	Southern Mississippi	216,742	78	Louisiana Tech	33,205
21	Texas Woman's	213,948	79	New School	32,294
22	Arkansas, Fayetteville	208,820	80	North Dakota State	30,862
23	Lehigh	199,758	81	Bowling Green State	28,706
24	Illinois State	196,679	82	Biola	25,664
25	Carnegie-Mellon	177,805	83	Claremont	21,871
26	Utah State	173,332	84	Wyoming	20,768
27	Missouri, Rolla	173,274	85	Maryland, Baltimore Ct.	18,651
28	Wisconsin, Milwaukee	164,799	86	SUNY Coll. Env. Sci. & For.	16,675
29	St. John's	161,991	87	Colorado, Denver	14,942
30	Texas, Arlington	155,297	88	Toledo	14,604
31	Rhode Island	150,989	89	Teachers College	9,162
32	Missouri, Kansas City	144,774	90	William and Mary	9,058
33	Tulsa	143,642	91	Montana State	7,667
34	Southern Methodist	143,395	92	U.S. International	4,100
35	Southwestern Louisiana	141,900	93	Idaho	3,688
36	Indiana State	136,722	94	Colorado School of Mines	838
37	San Francisco	134,535	95	Rockefeller	667
38	Wichita State	132,841	96	George Washington	0
39	South Dakota	128,775	97	Akron	U/A
40	Ohio	124,721	97	Andrews	U/A
41	Tufts	117,269	97	Calgary	U/A
42	Old Dominion	112,867	97	Calif. Institute of Tech.	U/A
43	Stevens Inst. of Tech.	108,505	97	Central Florida	U/A
44	American	107,563	97	Clemson	U/A
45	Alabama, Birmingham	106,915	97	Cleveland State	U/A
46	Tennessee Tech	105,857	97	DePaul	U/A
47	Texas, Dallas	100,564	97	Hahnemann	U/A
48	Northern Colorado	94,374	97	La Sierra	U/A
49	Memphis State	93,644	97	Middle Tennessee State	U/A
50	Portland State	93,627	97	Montreal	U/A
51	Clarkson	90,822	97	Nevada, Reno	U/A
52	South Dakota State	88,350	97	New Brunswick	U/A
53	Brandeis	87,896	97	New Hampshire	U/A
54	New Orleans	79,299	97	North Carolina, Greensboro	U/A
55	Polytechnic	75,453	97	Puerto Rico	U/A
56	Yeshiva	71,592	97	San Diego State	U/A
57	Calif., Santa Cruz	67,027	97	Windsor	U/A
58	Denver	66,657	116	Ottawa	N/A

U/A - Unavailable   N/A - Not Available

RANK ORDER TABLE 9
TOTAL LIBRARY EXPENDITURES

Rank	Institution	Value	Rank	Institution	Value
1	Montreal	13,764,572	59	Claremont	4,633,318
2	St. John's	11,200,639	60	Brandeis	4,598,263
3	Ohio	10,441,638	61	Rhode Island	4,585,470
4	Loyola, Chicago	9,871,944	62	Maine, Orono	4,550,724
5	Louisville	9,801,028	63	New Hampshire	4,508,232
6	South Florida	9,503,801	64	Calif. Institute of Tech.	4,391,563
7	Virginia Commonwealth	9,422,613	65	DePaul	4,353,787
8	Calif., Santa Cruz	8,670,303	66	Missouri, Kansas City	4,341,153
9	Ottawa	8,519,716	67	American	4,337,443
10	Georgia State	8,384,938	68	Tufts	4,315,663
11	Wake Forest	8,242,721	69	Florida Atlantic	4,085,226
12	Calgary	8,023,307	70	Old Dominion	3,972,790
13	Northern Illinois	8,003,300	71	Southern Mississippi	3,770,349
14	SUNY, Binghamton	7,776,318	72	Wichita State	3,717,554
15	Southern Methodist	7,728,841	73	Cleveland State	3,673,186
16	Northeastern	7,700,739	74	Indiana State	3,626,808
17	George Washington	7,424,864	75	Mississippi	3,621,062
18	St. Louis	7,331,498	76	Idaho	3,576,156
19	George Mason	7,258,839	77	Maryland, Baltimore Ct.	3,565,060
20	Puerto Rico	7,249,104	78	Catholic	3,553,972
21	San Diego State	7,061,958	79	Northern Colorado	3,553,508
22	William and Mary	7,013,329	80	Middle Tennessee State	3,524,042
23	Vermont	6,950,697	81	Tulsa	3,364,440
24	Alabama, Birmingham	6,889,238	82	Denver	3,314,953
25	Wisconsin, Milwaukee	6,854,346	83	Texas, Dallas	3,194,714
26	Miami, Ohio	6,800,033	84	Montana State	2,933,461
27	Bowling Green State	6,668,684	85	Missouri, St. Louis	2,812,150
28	Marquette	6,532,836	86	Hahnemann	2,806,881
29	Kansas State	6,459,392	87	Southwestern Louisiana	2,787,785
30	Fordham	6,380,634	88	New Orleans	2,713,219
31	Arkansas, Fayetteville	6,297,427	89	San Francisco	2,654,118
32	Ball State	6,269,378	90	Pepperdine	2,601,136
33	Nevada, Reno	6,134,595	91	North Dakota State	2,507,787
34	Central Florida	6,090,091	92	Idaho State	2,481,357
35	Akron	5,989,976	93	South Dakota State	2,349,711
36	Baylor	5,842,401	94	Texas Woman's	2,295,396
37	Clemson	5,801,700	95	Michigan Technological	2,210,680
38	Illinois State	5,721,825	96	South Dakota	2,207,185
39	Alaska	5,719,557	97	Tennessee Tech	2,117,126
40	Hofstra	5,630,830	98	Teachers College	2,091,771
41	Windsor	5,400,174	99	Andrews	1,903,651
42	Carnegie-Mellon	5,337,535	100	Louisiana Tech	1,870,449
43	North Texas	5,305,187	101	Missouri, Rolla	1,815,487
44	Colorado, Denver	5,199,423	102	Duquesne	1,753,318
45	Memphis State	5,160,655	103	Clark	1,734,987
46	Wyoming	5,148,702	104	East Texas State	1,732,767
47	New Mexico State	5,095,178	105	Pacific	1,729,989
48	Portland State	5,054,599	106	Drake	1,727,330
49	Toledo	4,980,183	107	New School	1,628,256
50	Northern Arizona	4,920,135	108	Colorado School of Mines	1,413,253
51	Yeshiva	4,875,145	109	Polytechnic	1,305,891
52	Utah State	4,843,344	110	Rockefeller	1,229,728
53	Texas, Arlington	4,811,824	111	Clarkson	1,187,429
54	Atlanta	4,805,254	112	SUNY Coll. Env. Sci. & For.	965,257
55	New Brunswick	4,777,009	113	La Sierra	927,904
56	Indiana/Purdue, Indianapolis	4,691,716	114	Biola	775,784
57	North Carolina, Greensboro	4,688,242	115	Stevens Inst. of Tech.	766,616
58	Lehigh	4,683,245	116	U.S. International	510,123

RANK ORDER TABLE 10
MONOGRAPHS PURCHASED

Rank	Institution	Value	Rank	Institution	Value
1	SUNY, Binghamton	34,429	59	Tulsa	8,314
2	South Florida	33,522	60	Northern Colorado	8,189
3	Virginia Commonwealth	33,329	61	Pacific	8,070
4	St. John's	32,494	62	Utah State	7,890
5	George Mason	30,769	63	Idaho State	7,039
6	Loyola, Chicago	29,271	64	Missouri, St. Louis	6,877
7	North Carolina, Greensboro	28,390	65	Andrews	6,842
8	Georgia State	26,482	66	Southwestern Louisiana	6,782
9	Northeastern	26,289	67	New School	6,480
10	Montreal	26,194	68	South Dakota	6,467
11	Akron	25,655	69	Catholic	6,309
12	Wake Forest	25,568	70	Florida Atlantic	6,286
13	Tufts	24,038	71	Clark	6,240
14	Miami, Ohio	22,913	72	East Texas State	5,899
15	Marquette	22,768	73	Rhode Island	5,447
16	Northern Arizona	21,853	74	Wyoming	5,094
17	Portland State	21,611	75	Texas, Arlington	4,503
18	American	20,549	76	Southern Mississippi	4,447
19	William and Mary	20,465	77	New Orleans	4,267
20	Brandeis	19,891	78	Montana State	3,979
21	Southern Methodist	19,842	79	Louisiana Tech	3,656
22	Wisconsin, Milwaukee	18,536	80	Texas Woman's	3,486
23	Ottawa	18,291	81	Missouri, Rolla	3,372
24	George Washington	17,840	82	North Dakota State	3,345
25	Denver	17,827	83	Duquesne	3,297
26	DePaul	17,581	84	La Sierra	2,993
27	Hofstra	17,369	85	Pepperdine	2,594
28	Middle Tennessee State	17,170	86	Biola	2,401
29	Ball State	16,819	87	Michigan Technological	2,214
30	Fordham	16,712	88	Hahnemann	2,209
31	North Texas	16,650	89	Teachers College	1,570
32	Arkansas, Fayetteville	16,461	90	Colorado School of Mines	1,410
33	Illinois State	16,390	91	SUNY Coll. Env. Sci. & For.	1,194
34	Northern Illinois	15,484	92	Stevens Inst. of Tech.	902
35	San Diego State	15,268	93	Rockefeller	856
36	Maine, Orono	15,181	94	Polytechnic	600
37	Kansas State	14,986	95	Alaska	U/A
38	Claremont	14,471	95	Baylor	U/A
39	Wichita State	14,433	95	Calgary	U/A
40	Atlanta	14,257	95	Calif. Institute of Tech.	U/A
41	St. Louis	14,226	95	Calif., Santa Cruz	U/A
42	Bowling Green State	14,113	95	Carnegie-Mellon	U/A
43	Clemson	13,989	95	Central Florida	U/A
44	Cleveland State	13,331	95	Clarkson	U/A
45	Alabama, Birmingham	13,126	95	Indiana/Purdue, Indianapolis	U/A
46	South Dakota State	12,982	95	Indiana State	U/A
47	San Francisco	12,820	95	Louisville	U/A
48	Nevada, Reno	12,354	95	Maryland, Baltimore Ct.	U/A
49	Colorado, Denver	12,124	95	Memphis State	U/A
50	Windsor	12,098	95	Mississippi	U/A
51	Lehigh	11,929	95	Ohio	U/A
52	New Mexico State	11,898	95	Old Dominion	U/A
53	Missouri, Kansas City	10,187	95	Tennessee Tech	U/A
54	Idaho	10,000	95	Texas, Dallas	U/A
55	New Hampshire	8,815	95	Toledo	U/A
56	Puerto Rico	8,600	95	U.S. International	U/A
57	New Brunswick	8,571	95	Vermont	U/A
58	Drake	8,500	95	Yeshiva	U/A

U/A - Unavailable

RANK ORDER TABLE 11
MONOGRAPHS EXPENDITURES

Rank	Institution	Value	Rank	Institution	Value
1	Central Florida	1,786,248	59	American	447,700
2	Georgia State	1,715,735	60	Maryland, Baltimore Ct.	442,953
3	Loyola, Chicago	1,323,416	61	Florida Atlantic	437,117
4	Virginia Commonwealth	1,321,331	62	Missouri, Kansas City	425,936
5	Ohio	1,267,374	63	South Dakota State	425,829
6	George Mason	1,235,826	64	Rhode Island	417,201
7	William and Mary	1,196,014	65	South Dakota	415,170
8	Northeastern	1,181,873	66	Windsor	414,601
9	Montreal	1,170,574	67	Colorado, Denver	405,185
10	South Florida	1,128,032	68	Yeshiva	377,863
11	Vermont	1,125,130	69	Andrews	365,177
12	Southern Methodist	1,069,308	70	Catholic	352,446
13	Marquette	1,062,864	71	Texas, Dallas	344,701
14	Louisville	1,007,138	72	New Mexico State	342,977
15	Akron	1,002,086	73	Memphis State	337,529
16	Northern Arizona	993,737	74	Texas, Arlington	337,130
17	SUNY, Binghamton	973,425	75	Clemson	331,636
18	Atlanta	956,932	76	New Brunswick	311,028
19	Nevada, Reno	952,658	77	Northern Colorado	294,326
20	Calif., Santa Cruz	944,673	78	Utah State	293,151
21	Baylor	921,480	79	Tulsa	285,557
22	Bowling Green State	896,939	80	Idaho	282,366
23	Fordham	828,533	81	Hahnemann	279,458
24	George Washington	814,662	82	Missouri, Rolla	275,036
25	Kansas State	799,624	83	Duquesne	271,372
26	Miami, Ohio	783,944	84	Idaho State	264,054
27	St. Louis	782,289	85	Cleveland State	261,544
28	Puerto Rico	773,052	86	Pacific	253,158
29	Middle Tennessee State	771,985	87	New Orleans	248,071
30	North Carolina, Greensboro	769,266	88	Southwestern Louisiana	245,955
31	Denver	743,106	89	Missouri, St. Louis	241,997
32	Toledo	735,177	90	North Texas	228,377
33	Wake Forest	727,420	91	Clark	218,951
34	Brandeis	721,951	92	Wyoming	211,485
35	Portland State	715,012	93	Tennessee Tech	200,214
36	DePaul	683,972	94	Calif. Institute of Tech.	199,427
37	Wisconsin, Milwaukee	676,253	95	Southern Mississippi	167,614
38	Claremont	670,888	96	North Dakota State	155,332
39	Arkansas, Fayetteville	662,866	97	New Hampshire	155,234
40	Indiana/Purdue, Indianapolis	661,917	98	New School	143,160
41	Calgary	656,567	99	East Texas State	139,331
42	Hofstra	644,192	100	Drake	124,347
43	Illinois State	629,004	101	Texas Woman's	121,347
44	Mississippi	620,300	102	La Sierra	118,144
45	Tufts	614,801	103	Pepperdine	114,275
46	Northern Illinois	613,311	104	Montana State	110,019
47	Maine, Orono	600,000	105	Louisiana Tech	103,100
48	St. John's	597,376	106	Michigan Technological	88,357
49	Alabama, Birmingham	594,949	107	Biola	88,060
50	San Diego State	579,447	108	SUNY Coll. Env. Sci. & For.	78,868
51	Ottawa	560,380	109	Colorado School of Mines	74,931
52	Lehigh	549,130	110	Stevens Inst. of Tech.	70,000
53	Old Dominion	540,944	111	Clarkson	61,474
54	Ball State	532,903	112	Polytechnic	56,100
55	Wichita State	515,684	113	Teachers College	53,965
56	Carnegie-Mellon	501,948	114	Rockefeller	52,176
57	San Francisco	498,978	115	U.S. International	48,082
58	Indiana State	453,012	116	Alaska	U/A

U/A - Unavailable

RANK ORDER TABLE 12
CURRENT SERIALS PURCHASED

Rank	Institution	Value	Rank	Institution	Value
1	St. John's	13,351	59	Pacific	2,480
2	St. Louis	12,457	60	Tufts	2,396
3	Mississippi	11,786	61	Clark	2,298
4	Arkansas, Fayetteville	11,170	62	South Dakota	2,252
5	Georgia State	9,909	63	Teachers College	2,203
6	Northern Illinois	9,434	64	San Francisco	2,187
7	William and Mary	9,424	65	Duquesne	1,886
8	George Washington	9,417	66	Atlanta	1,784
9	George Mason	9,246	67	Colorado School of Mines	1,457
10	Catholic	9,219	68	New School	1,215
11	SUNY, Binghamton	8,897	69	Missouri, Rolla	1,190
12	Northeastern	8,594	70	La Sierra	1,156
13	South Florida	8,372	71	SUNY Coll. Env. Sci. & For.	1,146
14	Marquette	8,074	72	Biola	922
15	Portland State	8,028	73	Rockefeller	453
16	Virginia Commonwealth	7,717	74	Akron	U/A
17	Clemson	7,180	74	Alaska	U/A
18	Tulsa	6,962	74	American	U/A
19	Kansas State	6,621	74	Andrews	U/A
20	Nevada, Reno	6,268	74	Ball State	U/A
21	Michigan Technological	6,260	74	Baylor	U/A
22	Maine, Orono	6,150	74	Bowling Green State	U/A
23	Puerto Rico	5,931	74	Calgary	U/A
24	New Hampshire	5,885	74	Calif. Institute of Tech.	U/A
25	New Mexico State	5,882	74	Calif., Santa Cruz	U/A
26	Claremont	5,799	74	Cleveland State	U/A
27	Southern Methodist	5,759	74	Colorado, Denver	U/A
28	Rhode Island	5,751	74	Denver	U/A
29	Memphis State	5,601	74	East Texas State	U/A
30	Idaho	5,526	74	Florida Atlantic	U/A
31	Lehigh	5,340	74	Fordham	U/A
32	Southwestern Louisiana	5,300	74	Hahnemann	U/A
33	Indiana State	5,170	74	Hofstra	U/A
34	Alabama, Birmingham	5,014	74	Louisville	U/A
35	San Diego State	4,990	74	Loyola, Chicago	U/A
36	North Carolina, Greensboro	4,978	74	Maryland, Baltimore Ct.	U/A
37	Toledo	4,942	74	Miami, Ohio	U/A
38	Illinois State	4,725	74	Middle Tennessee State	U/A
39	Central Florida	4,671	74	Missouri, Kansas City	U/A
40	Utah State	4,667	74	Montreal	U/A
41	Southern Mississippi	4,546	74	North Texas	U/A
42	DePaul	4,397	74	Northern Arizona	U/A
43	Brandeis	4,027	74	Northern Colorado	U/A
44	New Brunswick	3,969	74	Ohio	U/A
45	Indiana/Purdue, Indianapolis	3,946	74	Old Dominion	U/A
46	North Dakota State	3,836	74	Ottawa	U/A
47	Montana State	3,704	74	Pepperdine	U/A
48	Tennessee Tech	3,673	74	Polytechnic	U/A
49	Carnegie-Mellon	3,335	74	Stevens Inst. of Tech.	U/A
50	Missouri, St. Louis	3,300	74	Texas, Arlington	U/A
51	Wichita State	3,228	74	Texas, Dallas	U/A
52	Idaho State	3,209	74	U.S. International	U/A
53	New Orleans	3,205	74	Vermont	U/A
54	South Dakota State	3,024	74	Wake Forest	U/A
55	Drake	2,900	74	Windsor	U/A
56	Louisiana Tech	2,635	74	Wisconsin, Milwaukee	U/A
57	Texas Woman's	2,591	74	Wyoming	U/A
58	Clarkson	2,552	74	Yeshiva	U/A

U/A - Unavailable

RANK ORDER TABLE 13
CURRENT SERIALS EXPENDITURES

Rank	Institution	Value	Rank	Institution	Value
1	Montreal	3,215,682	59	Illinois State	1,049,977
2	Virginia Commonwealth	2,624,858	60	Tulsa	1,019,301
3	Louisville	2,616,138	61	San Diego State	1,009,985
4	Wake Forest	2,430,755	62	Old Dominion	1,009,576
5	South Florida	2,387,973	63	Michigan Technological	988,348
6	Loyola, Chicago	2,221,667	64	DePaul	986,635
7	Ottawa	2,185,782	65	North Carolina, Greensboro	980,000
8	Northeastern	2,181,033	66	Texas, Arlington	968,250
9	New Hampshire	2,133,047	67	Hofstra	932,590
10	Northern Illinois	2,053,889	68	Indiana/Purdue, Indianapolis	912,574
11	St. John's	2,053,262	69	Missouri, St. Louis	910,759
12	St. Louis	2,022,723	70	Northern Arizona	903,150
13	Arkansas, Fayetteville	2,001,158	71	Southwestern Louisiana	902,788
14	Calgary	1,998,259	72	Ball State	877,883
15	Marquette	1,974,432	73	Baylor	867,339
16	Vermont	1,974,185	74	Colorado, Denver	859,809
17	Wyoming	1,938,086	75	Middle Tennessee State	854,187
18	Clemson	1,903,020	76	North Dakota State	848,670
19	SUNY, Binghamton	1,867,083	77	Denver	823,032
20	George Mason	1,807,668	78	New Brunswick	817,435
21	Alabama, Birmingham	1,773,868	79	Missouri, Kansas City	814,584
22	Kansas State	1,772,022	80	Hahnemann	803,804
23	William and Mary	1,760,014	81	New Orleans	795,918
24	Maine, Orono	1,760,000	82	Indiana State	782,646
25	Georgia State	1,734,759	83	Wichita State	781,713
26	Ohio	1,722,326	84	Texas, Dallas	764,715
27	Calif. Institute of Tech.	1,679,033	85	South Dakota State	733,128
28	George Washington	1,639,923	86	American	731,762
29	Lehigh	1,634,510	87	Florida Atlantic	717,571
30	Southern Methodist	1,605,725	88	Catholic	702,830
31	Memphis State	1,582,616	89	Idaho State	688,063
32	Akron	1,531,592	90	Tennessee Tech	684,622
33	Nevada, Reno	1,490,615	91	Northern Colorado	617,558
34	Puerto Rico	1,474,147	92	Louisiana Tech	594,065
35	Wisconsin, Milwaukee	1,458,382	93	Atlanta	585,795
36	Calif., Santa Cruz	1,436,857	94	Colorado School of Mines	530,695
37	Mississippi	1,409,247	95	Drake	514,459
38	Utah State	1,398,379	96	Alaska	478,687
39	Fordham	1,379,709	97	Missouri, Rolla	478,233
40	Yeshiva	1,373,846	98	Clarkson	474,086
41	Rhode Island	1,356,590	99	Clark	466,724
42	Portland State	1,306,670	100	Pepperdine	456,650
43	New Mexico State	1,302,026	101	South Dakota	455,979
44	Cleveland State	1,219,923	102	Pacific	418,926
45	Miami, Ohio	1,219,291	103	Rockefeller	396,088
46	Claremont	1,203,256	104	San Francisco	383,228
47	Montana State	1,191,820	105	SUNY Coll. Env. Sci. & For.	372,412
48	Maryland, Baltimore Ct.	1,165,282	106	Duquesne	357,746
49	Carnegie-Mellon	1,156,510	107	Texas Woman's	311,145
50	Bowling Green State	1,152,108	108	East Texas State	305,342
51	Central Florida	1,142,187	109	Polytechnic	285,550
52	Brandeis	1,134,516	110	Andrews	240,516
53	Idaho	1,129,503	111	Teachers College	220,780
54	Tufts	1,117,524	112	Biola	146,701
55	Toledo	1,112,699	113	U.S. International	129,975
56	Windsor	1,099,826	114	La Sierra	129,496
57	North Texas	1,099,574	115	New School	120,054
58	Southern Mississippi	1,075,358	116	Stevens Inst. of Tech.	17,610

RANK ORDER TABLE 14
TOTAL ITEMS LOANED

Rank	Institution	Value	Rank	Institution	Value
1	Northern Illinois	84,711	59	Bowling Green State	9,658
2	DePaul	52,737	60	Portland State	9,460
3	Illinois State	48,125	61	Utah State	9,059
4	Miami, Ohio	47,838	62	St. John's	8,988
5	Maine, Orono	42,121	63	South Dakota State	8,977
6	Loyola, Chicago	39,045	64	Marquette	8,733
7	Akron	36,767	65	Missouri, Kansas City	8,688
8	Virginia Commonwealth	27,919	66	Idaho State	8,525
9	South Florida	26,181	67	Fordham	8,519
10	Ball State	26,180	68	Yeshiva	8,417
11	Colorado, Denver	24,505	69	Maryland, Baltimore Ct.	8,211
12	Wyoming	22,849	70	Texas, Dallas	7,795
13	Alabama, Birmingham	22,797	71	Clark	7,413
14	Ottawa	20,548	72	Lehigh	7,355
15	North Texas	20,335	73	North Carolina, Greensboro	7,341
16	Idaho	20,256	74	Brandeis	7,305
17	Kansas State	20,019	75	Catholic	7,253
18	Indiana/Purdue, Indianapolis	19,194	76	Calif., Santa Cruz	7,093
19	Ohio	18,647	77	Wisconsin, Milwaukee	6,726
20	SUNY, Binghamton	17,973	78	South Dakota	6,641
21	Montreal	17,509	79	Old Dominion	6,483
22	Northern Arizona	16,635	80	Missouri, Rolla	6,099
23	Northeastern	16,588	81	New Brunswick	6,088
24	Toledo	16,517	82	Denver	6,086
25	Rhode Island	16,325	83	Southwestern Louisiana	5,993
26	Wake Forest	16,063	84	Carnegie-Mellon	5,927
27	Northern Colorado	15,774	85	Tulsa	5,559
28	Central Florida	15,771	86	Pacific	5,449
29	Indiana State	15,678	87	Drake	5,395
30	Baylor	15,284	88	Tennessee Tech	5,286
31	George Mason	14,876	89	Atlanta	4,915
32	St. Louis	14,733	90	Windsor	4,588
33	Calgary	14,346	91	Middle Tennessee State	4,487
34	Georgia State	14,095	92	Colorado School of Mines	4,289
35	William and Mary	14,076	93	Southern Mississippi	4,209
36	Texas, Arlington	13,555	94	Tufts	4,154
37	Montana State	13,544	95	Memphis State	3,752
38	George Washington	13,272	96	Claremont	3,357
39	Southern Methodist	13,263	97	New Orleans	3,263
40	East Texas State	13,094	98	SUNY Coll. Env. Sci. & For.	3,231
41	Vermont	12,530	99	Calif. Institute of Tech.	3,213
42	American	12,267	100	Michigan Technological	3,150
43	Texas Woman's	12,186	101	Hofstra	2,921
44	North Dakota State	12,130	102	Andrews	2,893
45	Florida Atlantic	12,127	103	Louisiana Tech	2,835
46	Missouri, St. Louis	12,011	104	Clarkson	2,704
47	New Mexico State	11,976	105	Rockefeller	2,248
48	San Diego State	11,925	106	San Francisco	2,052
49	Wichita State	11,888	107	Duquesne	1,597
50	Cleveland State	11,836	108	Teachers College	1,289
51	Hahnemann	11,795	109	Biola	1,180
52	Arkansas, Fayetteville	11,591	110	Pepperdine	768
53	Mississippi	11,049	111	La Sierra	734
54	Louisville	10,944	112	Puerto Rico	714
55	Nevada, Reno	10,557	113	Stevens Inst. of Tech.	623
56	Alaska	10,474	114	U.S. International	395
57	Clemson	10,326	115	New School	342
58	New Hampshire	9,796	116	Polytechnic	339

U/A - Unavailable   N/A - Not Applicable

RANK ORDER TABLE 15
TOTAL ITEMS BORROWED

Rank	Institution	Value	Rank	Institution	Value
1	Northern Illinois	57,517	59	Northern Colorado	7,874
2	DePaul	28,946	60	Hahnemann	7,847
3	Akron	28,141	61	Georgia State	7,647
4	George Washington	24,837	62	Carnegie-Mellon	7,558
5	Miami, Ohio	24,435	63	Montreal	7,501
6	North Dakota State	19,714	64	Brandeis	7,499
7	Maine, Orono	18,456	65	Indiana State	7,012
8	Missouri, Kansas City	17,895	66	Tufts	6,899
9	Kansas State	17,806	67	Memphis State	6,726
10	Loyola, Chicago	17,060	68	William and Mary	6,686
11	San Diego State	16,382	69	Clark	6,667
12	Texas, Arlington	16,152	70	Maryland, Baltimore Ct.	6,537
13	Ohio	15,768	71	Denver	6,526
14	St. Louis	15,629	72	Toledo	6,485
15	South Florida	15,120	73	Hofstra	6,473
16	Calgary	15,050	74	Wake Forest	6,460
17	New Mexico State	14,921	75	Idaho State	6,378
18	Illinois State	14,176	76	South Dakota	6,261
19	Arkansas, Fayetteville	13,940	77	Northeastern	6,185
20	Indiana/Purdue, Indianapolis	13,765	78	Windsor	6,177
21	Texas Woman's	13,757	79	Mississippi	6,140
22	Idaho	13,490	80	Pacific	6,027
23	Ball State	13,288	81	Nevada, Reno	5,966
24	Claremont	12,766	82	Southern Methodist	5,865
25	Rhode Island	12,076	83	Stevens Inst. of Tech.	5,530
26	George Mason	12,069	84	Bowling Green State	5,428
27	Cleveland State	12,062	85	Michigan Technological	5,310
28	Central Florida	11,849	86	Old Dominion	5,020
29	Florida Atlantic	11,561	87	Fordham	4,962
30	Wichita State	11,420	88	Baylor	4,904
31	SUNY, Binghamton	11,122	89	Southern Mississippi	4,884
32	Montana State	11,111	90	East Texas State	4,846
33	Wisconsin, Milwaukee	11,078	91	New Orleans	4,630
34	Clemson	11,074	92	North Carolina, Greensboro	4,592
35	Colorado, Denver	10,894	93	Catholic	4,552
36	Alabama, Birmingham	10,821	94	Clarkson	4,512
37	Wyoming	10,794	95	Atlanta	4,462
38	Calif., Santa Cruz	10,786	96	Drake	4,297
39	Missouri, Rolla	10,653	97	Portland State	4,131
40	Missouri, St. Louis	10,428	98	Louisiana Tech	3,878
41	Calif. Institute of Tech.	10,249	99	Tennessee Tech	3,642
42	North Texas	10,223	100	San Francisco	3,576
43	Utah State	9,767	101	St. John's	3,365
44	Virginia Commonwealth	9,696	102	Colorado School of Mines	3,314
45	Vermont	9,484	103	Middle Tennessee State	3,119
46	Yeshiva	9,439	104	Southwestern Louisiana	3,103
47	Marquette	9,409	105	Andrews	2,636
48	Alaska	9,204	106	Polytechnic	2,189
49	South Dakota State	9,112	107	Rockefeller	2,173
50	Northern Arizona	9,033	108	Puerto Rico	1,766
51	New Brunswick	8,981	109	Teachers College	1,567
52	Tulsa	8,883	110	SUNY Coll. Env. Sci. & For.	1,373
53	Lehigh	8,789	111	Duquesne	1,176
54	New Hampshire	8,610	112	Biola	889
55	Texas, Dallas	8,486	113	Pepperdine	804
56	Louisville	8,454	114	La Sierra	275
57	American	8,229	115	U.S. International	231
58	Ottawa	8,145	116	New School	210

RANK ORDER TABLE 16
PROFESSIONAL STAFF (FTE)

Rank	Institution	Value	Rank	Institution	Value
1	Montreal	81	58	Northern Arizona	27
2	Ohio	60	60	Colorado, Denver	26
3	South Florida	59	60	Florida Atlantic	26
4	Hahnemann	57	60	Nevada, Reno	26
4	St. Louis	57	60	New Orleans	26
6	Puerto Rico	56	64	Portland State	25
6	Southern Methodist	56	64	Tufts	25
8	Bowling Green State	51	64	Tulsa	25
8	Loyola, Chicago	51	67	Middle Tennessee State	24
10	Wyoming	50	67	Mississippi	24
11	Ottawa	49	67	New Brunswick	24
12	Northern Illinois	45	67	North Carolina, Greensboro	24
13	Alabama, Birmingham	42	71	Atlanta	23
13	Arkansas, Fayetteville	42	71	Idaho	23
13	Kansas State	42	71	Maine, Orono	23
13	Louisville	42	71	Missouri, St. Louis	23
17	Georgia State	41	71	New Hampshire	23
17	Marquette	41	71	Old Dominion	23
17	Utah State	41	71	Wichita State	23
17	Virginia Commonwealth	41	78	Texas, Dallas	22
17	Wisconsin, Milwaukee	41	79	American	21
22	Ball State	40	79	Cleveland State	21
22	Miami, Ohio	40	81	Lehigh	19
24	Akron	39	81	Rhode Island	19
25	Illinois State	38	83	Claremont	18
25	Northeastern	38	83	Denver	18
27	Texas, Arlington	37	83	Northern Colorado	18
28	Fordham	36	86	Montana State	17
28	George Mason	36	86	North Dakota State	17
28	Hofstra	36	86	Texas Woman's	17
28	Missouri, Kansas City	36	89	East Texas State	16
28	North Texas	36	89	Michigan Technological	16
28	SUNY, Binghamton	36	89	Southwestern Louisiana	16
28	St. John's	36	92	Duquesne	15
35	Calgary	35	92	Louisiana Tech	15
35	Indiana/Purdue, Indianapolis	35	92	Maryland, Baltimore Ct.	15
35	Wake Forest	35	92	Pepperdine	15
38	Alaska	34	92	Tennessee Tech	15
39	Carnegie-Mellon	33	97	Calif. Institute of Tech.	14
39	Central Florida	33	97	South Dakota State	14
39	William and Mary	33	99	Idaho State	13
42	Baylor	32	99	San Francisco	13
42	Clemson	32	101	Andrews	12
42	New Mexico State	32	101	Clark	12
45	San Diego State	31	101	Polytechnic	12
46	Brandeis	30	101	South Dakota	12
46	Catholic	30	105	New School	11
46	Toledo	30	105	Pacific	11
46	Vermont	30	107	Drake	10
50	George Washington	29	108	Missouri, Rolla	9
50	Indiana State	29	109	Colorado School of Mines	7
50	Teachers College	29	109	SUNY Coll. Env. Sci. & For.	7
50	Windsor	29	111	La Sierra	6
54	DePaul	28	111	Stevens Inst. of Tech.	6
54	Memphis State	28	113	Biola	5
54	Southern Mississippi	28	113	Clarkson	5
54	Yeshiva	28	113	U.S. International	5
58	Calif., Santa Cruz	27	116	Rockefeller	3

Rank	Institution	Value	Rank	Institution	Value
1	Montreal	218	57	Indiana State	43
2	Puerto Rico	167	57	Old Dominion	43
3	Calgary	161	61	Akron	42
4	Ottawa	144	61	Northeastern	42
5	South Florida	108	61	Toledo	42
6	George Washington	107	64	George Mason	41
7	Northern Illinois	96	64	Rhode Island	41
8	Louisville	95	66	Denver	40
9	Georgia State	91	67	Maryland, Baltimore Ct.	39
10	Virginia Commonwealth	89	67	Southern Mississippi	39
11	Illinois State	83	69	Catholic	38
12	Ball State	82	69	Tulsa	38
12	SUNY, Binghamton	82	71	Texas, Dallas	37
14	Loyola, Chicago	79	71	Wyoming	37
14	Memphis State	79	73	Idaho	35
16	Baylor	75	73	Lehigh	35
17	New Brunswick	74	75	Tufts	34
18	Ohio	73	76	Atlanta	33
18	St. Louis	73	76	Brandeis	33
20	Clemson	70	76	Montana State	33
20	Vermont	70	76	Northern Colorado	33
20	Windsor	70	76	Wichita State	33
23	San Diego State	69	81	Cleveland State	32
24	Arkansas, Fayetteville	68	81	Missouri, St. Louis	32
24	North Texas	68	83	Southwestern Louisiana	31
26	Calif., Santa Cruz	65	83	Texas Woman's	31
27	Alabama, Birmingham	64	85	Middle Tennessee State	30
27	St. John's	64	85	New Orleans	30
27	Wake Forest	64	87	DePaul	28
30	Kansas State	63	87	North Dakota State	28
31	Colorado, Denver	62	89	Idaho State	27
31	Hofstra	62	89	Mississippi	27
33	Texas, Arlington	61	91	Utah State	26
34	Hahnemann	60	92	East Texas State	24
34	Southern Methodist	60	93	Tennessee Tech	20
36	New Hampshire	59	94	Pacific	19
37	New Mexico State	55	95	Duquesne	18
37	William and Mary	55	95	Pepperdine	18
39	North Carolina, Greensboro	54	95	San Francisco	18
40	Central Florida	53	95	South Dakota	18
40	Marquette	53	99	Michigan Technological	17
40	Northern Arizona	53	99	South Dakota State	17
40	Wisconsin, Milwaukee	53	101	Louisiana Tech	16
44	Miami, Ohio	52	101	Missouri, Rolla	16
45	Bowling Green State	51	103	Clark	15
45	Carnegie-Mellon	51	103	Drake	15
47	Florida Atlantic	50	103	New School	15
47	Nevada, Reno	50	103	Teachers College	15
49	American	49	107	Andrews	14
49	Missouri, Kansas City	49	108	Colorado School of Mines	11
51	Fordham	47	109	Rockefeller	9
51	Maine, Orono	47	109	U.S. International	9
51	Yeshiva	47	111	Biola	8
54	Portland State	46	111	Clarkson	8
55	Indiana/Purdue, Indianapolis	45	111	La Sierra	8
56	Alaska	44	114	SUNY Coll. Env. Sci. & For.	6
57	Calif. Institute of Tech.	43	115	Polytechnic	5
57	Claremont	43	116	Stevens Inst. of Tech.	4

RANK ORDER TABLE 18
TOTAL STAFF (FTE)

Rank	Institution	Value	Rank	Institution	Value
1	Puerto Rico	305	58	Indiana State	102
2	Montreal	299	60	Portland State	99
3	South Florida	222	61	Florida Atlantic	98
4	Loyola, Chicago	221	61	Maine, Orono	98
5	Calgary	215	63	DePaul	96
6	Ohio	207	64	Old Dominion	95
7	Northern Illinois	200	65	Catholic	94
8	Ottawa	193	66	Brandeis	93
9	San Diego State	190	66	Northern Colorado	93
10	Illinois State	186	68	Southern Mississippi	92
11	Northeastern	185	69	Rhode Island	91
12	Louisville	183	70	Cleveland State	82
13	Georgia State	173	71	Duquesne	81
14	Hahnemann	169	72	Mississippi	80
15	Miami, Ohio	168	73	Middle Tennessee State	78
16	Ball State	167	74	Idaho	77
17	Central Florida	165	75	Wichita State	76
17	North Texas	165	76	Lehigh	75
19	SUNY, Binghamton	159	76	Tufts	75
20	Southern Methodist	157	76	Yeshiva	75
20	St. Louis	157	79	New Orleans	74
22	Bowling Green State	156	79	Texas Woman's	74
23	Virginia Commonwealth	155	81	Atlanta	71
24	Arkansas, Fayetteville	154	81	Maryland, Baltimore Ct.	71
25	George Washington	153	81	Missouri, St. Louis	71
26	Akron	152	81	Tulsa	71
26	Alabama, Birmingham	152	85	Denver	69
28	Baylor	150	86	North Dakota State	68
29	Kansas State	144	87	Teachers College	63
30	Texas, Arlington	139	88	Calif. Institute of Tech.	61
30	Wisconsin, Milwaukee	139	88	Claremont	61
32	Northern Arizona	133	88	East Texas State	61
33	Calif., Santa Cruz	130	88	Idaho State	61
34	Marquette	129	92	Southwestern Louisiana	60
34	Wake Forest	129	93	Texas, Dallas	59
36	New Mexico State	128	94	Montana State	56
36	Vermont	128	95	Louisiana Tech	54
38	Clemson	124	96	Tennessee Tech	52
39	Nevada, Reno	123	97	Pacific	47
40	Memphis State	121	98	Andrews	45
40	Toledo	121	99	Michigan Technological	44
42	Fordham	120	100	Pepperdine	43
42	Missouri, Kansas City	120	101	South Dakota State	42
44	New Hampshire	119	102	Clark	41
45	St. John's	118	102	Drake	41
46	Hofstra	116	104	South Dakota	39
46	Windsor	116	105	San Francisco	36
48	Indiana/Purdue, Indianapolis	111	106	Missouri, Rolla	29
48	Wyoming	111	106	New School	29
50	Alaska	110	108	Colorado School of Mines	26
50	Carnegie-Mellon	110	109	Polytechnic	22
50	William and Mary	110	110	Clarkson	21
53	George Mason	106	110	La Sierra	21
53	Utah State	106	112	Biola	20
55	Colorado, Denver	105	112	Stevens Inst. of Tech.	20
55	North Carolina, Greensboro	105	114	U.S. International	17
57	New Brunswick	104	115	SUNY Coll. Env. Sci. & For.	15
58	American	102	116	Rockefeller	12

1994-95 COMPILER'S NOTES

The 1994-95 ACRL University Library Statistics publication was prepared by the Library Research Center of the University of Illinois Graduate School of Library and Information Science.

The procedures for preparing the 1994-95 statistics were largely patterned on those used in previous compilations. The compilation of the 1994-95 statistics presented inconsistencies similar to those encountered in previous years. Every effort was made to minimize obvious errors and to increase the accuracy of the data presented. Where necessary, follow-up telephone calls were made or facsimiles sent to verify the data reported by individual libraries.

Three types of checks for inconsistencies in the data were conducted:

(1) Errors due to misunderstanding the instructions for completing the questionnaire.

(2) Errors due to miscalculations; there are several items in the survey where respondents are asked to calculate figures based on their responses to previous questions.

(3) Discrepancies in the figures reported by the libraries this year in comparison to the figures reported in either the 1990-91 or the 1992-93 compilation.

By examining the consistency of an institution's responses from year-to-year, obvious errata in reporting were discovered. Follow-up calls to libraries verified and corrected these inconsistencies. If the figures were correct as reported but further explanation was needed, these remarks were added to the libraries' footnotes.

Corrections were made after the institutions were contacted, unless it was an obvious minor mathematical miscalculation. In a few instances the institutions could not be contacted despite repeated callbacks and thus limited inconsistencies may remain in the data file. Because the data are available in machine readable form it is relatively easy to make corrections. Anyone noticing errors in the data is asked to bring them to the attention of ACRL.

Coding Procedures

The institutional variables were checked for logical relations; follow-up telephone calls were made whenever the number of graduate students (part-time and full-time) exceeded the total number of students (undergraduate plus graduate, part-time and full-time respectively). Prior to the 1992-93 compilation, it was not customary to verify the institutional figures by telephone since they are available in the IPEDS survey of the Department of Education. However, when this inconsistency was found, it was decided that the Library Research Center would verify that the figures reported for total part-time and full-time students include both graduate and undergraduate students. Researchers are encouraged to review the consistency of the figures reported in the ACRL data set with those reported in the IPEDS survey.

A library that reports expenditure figures which add up to total library expenditures and has left a blank for some of the expenditures categories has been assigned a code of "U/A" for the expenditures categories that are blank. A modification from previous compilations was made in that libraries reporting "N/A" for materials expenditures were left as "N/A," not recoded as "0."

In reporting current serials purchased and current serials received but not purchased a number of libraries confused U/A (unavailable) and N/A (not applicable). For serials received but not purchased the "N/A" response was changed to "U/A" if serials received could not be disaggregated from serials purchased.

If a library reported "N/A" in a category where "N/A" is inappropriate (such as faculty or total operating expenditures) then "N/A" was coded as "U/A."

Canadian libraries were asked to report their expenditures in Canadian dollars. So that an accurate basis for comparison could be achieved, Canadian libraries' expenditures were converted to U.S. dollars at the rate of 1.3794 Canadian dollars to one U.S. dollar. This is the average monthly noon exchange rate published in the Bank of Canada *Review* for the period July 1994 to June 1995.

Changes in the ACRL instrument

The instrument used for the ACRL survey is based on the form used by the ARL. This year, the format of numbering the questions changed, and six additional variables were added to the questionnaire.

Variables included for the first time in the 1994-95 ACRL survey are: presentations to library groups, participants in group presentations, reference transactions, initial circulations, total circulations, and reserve circulations. Since these variables appear for the first time, a number of libraries were unable to report their statistics on these activities; however, it is anticipated that reporting of figures for the new variables will improve in the future.

The rank order tables for the Computer Files, Manuscripts and Archives, Cartographic, Graphic, Audio, and Film and Video categories were not included in this publication. Rather, this information was integrated into the Library Data Tables, as are the data for the new variables. This organization reflects the changes made to the ARL format and followed by the ACRL.

Footnotes to the ACRL statistics report considerable information about each library. This kind of information is useful in clarifying the reported figures, and illustrates the degree to which certain libraries can be compared with others. There was minimal editorial intervention in transcribing the text. Obvious grammatical errors were corrected, and the order of the comments was occasionally modified for consistency and clarity. The goal was to reproduce the language of the original comments as faithfully as possible. In the past, the footnotes referred to columns on the Library Data Tables. This year, they are numbered according to the question to which they refer on the original questionnaire.

For the first time, statistics for the ACRL report were collected on computer diskettes. The questionnaire was programmed in LRC-QUERY, a software package the enables construction of customized, user-friendly programs for computer administration of any survey. Libraries received LRC-QUERY on a standard computer diskette, containing a facsimile of the survey form with extensive instructions on the use of the program and basic computer tasks, to enable even an inexperienced computer user to complete the survey with relative ease. There was considerable success in this effort, as only sixteen institutions deferred to the paper version of the survey. (All libraries received both paper and electronic versions of the survey.)

Machine readable data file

The statistical data compile by the LRC for ACRL are available in machine readable form. The computer disk presents the data file in a variety of formats. Detailed information as to the location of the variables, are provided in the README file on the disk. Contact the ACRL office for more information: (800) 545-2433 or (312) 280-2517.

This form is provided for reference. It need not be completed unless you are unable to complete the electronic ACRL provided on diskette.

ACRL STATISTICS QUESTIONNAIRE, 1994-95*

Reporting Institution _____ Date Returned to ACRL _____

Questionnaire Completed by (Name) _____

Position _____ Phone _____

Contact Person (if different) _____

Position _____ Phone _____

Please do not leave any lines blank. If an exact figure is unavailable, **use -1, i.e. "U/A."** If a question is not applicable in your library, **use -2, i.e. "N/A."** If the appropriate answer is zero or none, use "0".

COLLECTIONS

Volumes in Library: *(See instruction Q1-4)*

1. *Volumes held June on 30, 1994*
   (Exclude microforms, uncataloged govt. docs., maps, a/v material.
   Record figure reported last year or footnote adjusted figure on p. 4.)   _____

2a. Volumes added during year -- Gross *(See instruction Q2)*
   (Exclude microforms, uncataloged govt. docs., maps, a/v material.)   _____

2b. *Volumes withdrawn during year*
   (Exclude microforms, uncataloged govt. docs., maps, a/v material.)   _____

2c. Volumes added during year -- Net (Subtract line 2b from line 2a)   _____

3. Volumes held on June 30, 1995 (Add line 1 to line 2c)   _____

4. Number of monographic volumes purchased *(See instruction Q4)*
   (Volumes for which expenditures are reported on line 16. Footnote if titles.)   _____

Serials: *(See instruction Q5-7)*

5. Number of current serials, including periodicals, <u>purchased</u>   _____

6. Number of current serials, including periodicals, <u>received but not</u>
   <u>purchased</u> (Exchanges, gifts, deposits, etc.) *(See instruction Q6)*   _____

7. Total number of current serials received (Add line 5 to line 6)   _____

Modified from the <u>ARL Statistics 1994-95</u> by permission of the Association of Research Libraries (ARL).

COLLECTIONS (cont'd.)

Other Library Materials: Total number of pieces held on June 30, 1995:

8. Microform units *(See instruction Q8)*   _____

9. Government documents not counted elsewhere *(See instruction Q9)*   _____

10. Computer files *(See instruction Q10)*   _____

11. Manuscripts and archives (linear ft.) *(See instruction Q11)*   _____

Audiovisual materials:

12. Cartographic
    (See instruction Q12) _____

13. Graphic
    (See instruction Q13) _____

14. Audio
    (See instruction Q14) _____

15. Film and Video
    (See instruction Q15) _____

EXPENDITURES *(See instruction Q16-27)*   Reported in Canadian dollars?   Yes _____ No _____

Library Materials:

16. Monographs (Expenditures for volumes reported on line 4) *(See instruction Q16)*   _____

17. Current serials including periodicals *(See instruction Q17)*   _____

18. Other library materials (e.g., microforms, a/v, etc.) *(See instruction Q18)*   _____

19. Miscellaneous (All materials fund expenditures not included above)
    (See instruction Q19)   _____

20. Total library materials (Add lines 16, 17, 18, 19)   _____

21. **Contract binding:** *(See instruction Q21)*   _____

Salaries and Wages: *(See instruction Q22-25)*

22. Professional staff   _____

23. Support staff   _____

24. Student assistants *(See instruction Q24-25)*   _____

25. Total salaries and wages (Add lines 22, 23, 24)   _____

26. **Other operating expenditures:** *(See instruction Q26)*   _____

27. **Total library expenditures:** (Add lines 20, 21, 25, 26)   _____

PERSONNEL *(See instruction Q28-31. Round figures to nearest whole number.)*

    28. Professional staff, FTE *(See instruction Q28)*   _____

    29. Support staff, FTE   _____

    30. Student assistants, FTE *(See instruction Q30)*   _____

    31. Total FTE staff (Add lines 28, 29, 30)   _____

INSTRUCTION *(See instruction Q32-33)*

    32. Number of library presentations to groups *(See instruction Q32)*   _____

    33. Number of total participants in group presentations reported on line 32
        (See instruction Q33)   _____

REFERENCE

    34. Number of reference transactions *(See instruction Q34)*   _____

CIRCULATION *(See instruction Q35-37)*

    35. Number of initial circulations (excluding reserves)   _____

    36. Total circulations (initial and renewals, excluding reserves)   _____

    37. Number of reserve circulations *(See instruction Q37)*   _____

INTERLIBRARY LOANS *(See instruction Q38-39)*

    38. Total number of filled requests for materials **provided** to other libraries   _____

    39. Total number of filled requests for materials **received** from other libraries   _____

PH.D. DEGREES *(See instruction Q40-41)*

    40. Number of Ph.D.s awarded in FY1994-95   _____

    41. Number of fields in which Ph.D.s can be awarded *(See instruction Q41)*   _____

FACULTY *(See instruction Q42)*

    42. Number of full-time instructional faculty in FY1994-95   _____

ENROLLMENT -- FALL 1994 (TOTALS) *(See instruction Q43-46; here, line numbers refer to IPEDS survey form)*

    43. Full-time students (Add line 8, columns 15 & 16, and line 14, cols. 15 & 16)   _____

    44. Part-time students (Add line 22, columns 15 & 16, and line 28, cols. 15 & 16)   _____

    45. Full-time graduate students (Line 14, columns 15 & 16)   _____

    46. Part-time graduate students (Line 28, columns 15 & 16)   _____

LOCAL CHARACTERISTICS or **ATTRIBUTES**

    47. Basis of volume count is: _____ Physical   _____ Bibliographic

    48. Government documents are included in count of Current Serials.   _____ Yes   _____ No

    49. Fringe benefits are included in expenditures for salaries and wages.   _____ Yes   _____ No

    50. Law Library statistics are included.   _____ Yes   _____ No   _____ We do not have a Law Library

    51. Medical Library statistics are included.   _____ Yes   _____ No   _____ We do not have a Medical Library

    52. Other <u>main</u> campus libraries included: [list in "Footnotes" below].

    53. Branch Campus Libraries. *(See paragraph six of the "General Instructions")*

        Figures include branch CAMPUS libraries: _____ Yes   _____ No   _____ We have only one campus.

        If branch campus libraries are included, please specify which campuses in "Footnotes" below.

        If branch campus libraries are <u>not</u> included, please specify which campuses in "Footnotes" below.

FOOTNOTES *(See instruction Q54)*

PLEASE RETURN COMPLETED QUESTIONNAIRE AND EVALUATION TO THE LRC OFFICE BY **DECEMBER 15, 1995.**

Library Research Center, University of Illinois, Library and Information Science Building, 501 East Daniel Street, Champaign, IL 61820. (217) 333-1980. Please call Diane LaBarbera for assistance with the questionnaire.

ACRL STATISTICS, 1994-95
Instructions for Completing the Questionnaire

General Instructions

Please enter your data on the ACRL Questionnaire diskette, if possible. The printed copy of the questionnaire is a worksheet provided for your convenience. <u>Be sure to read all of the instructions regarding the use of the program as well as these instructions before beginning to input your data.</u>

Definitions of the statistical categories used in this questionnaire can be found in *American National Standard for Library and Information Science and Related Publishing Practices - Library Statistics. Z39.7-1983*. (New York, American National Standards Institute, 1983.) The questionnaire assumes a fiscal year ending June 30,1995. If your fiscal year is different, please provide a footnote in the "Footnotes" section of the questionnaire.

Please do not use decimals. All figures should be rounded to the nearest whole number.

Please do not leave any lines blank. If an exact figure is UnAvailable, use **-1**, i.e. "U/A". If a question is Not Applicable to your library, use **-2**, i.e. "N/A". If the appropriate answer is zero or none, use "0."

In a university that includes both main and branch campuses, <u>an effort should be made to report figures for the main campus only</u>. (The U.S. National Center for Education Statistics, Integrated Postsecondary Education Data System (IPEDS) defines a **branch campus** as one "located in a community different from that of its parent institution...beyond a reasonable commuting distance from the main campus...The educational activities at the location must be organized on a relatively permanent basis...and include course offerings for one or more complete college-level programs of at least one full year.") If figures for libraries located on branch campuses are reported, please explain in a footnote in the "Footnotes" section of the questionnaire.

A **branch library** is defined as an auxiliary library service outlet with quarters separate from the central library of a system, which has a basic collection of books and other materials, a regular staffing level, and an established schedule. A branch library is administered <u>either</u> by the central library <u>or</u> (as in the case of some law and medical libraries) through the administrative structure of other units within the university. Departmental study/reading rooms are not included.

Specific Instructions

Questions 1-4. Collections. Use the ANSI Z39.7-1983 definition for **volume** as follows:

A physical unit of any printed, typewritten, handwritten, mimeographed, or processed work, contained in one binding or portfolio, hardbound or paperbound, that has been cataloged, classified, and made ready for use.

Includes duplicates and bound volumes of periodicals. For purposes of this questionnaire, unclassified bound serials arrange in alphabetical order are considered classified. Exclude microforms, maps, nonprint materials, and uncatalogued items. If any of these items cannot be excluded, please provide an explanatory footnote in the "Footnotes" section of the questionnaire.

<u>Include government document volumes that are accessible through the library's catalogs regardless of whether they are separately shelved</u>. "Classified" includes documents arranged by Superintendent of Documents, CODOC, or similar numbers. "Cataloged" includes documents for which records are provided by the library or downloaded from other sources into the library's card or online catalogs. Documents should, to the extent possible, be counted as they would if they were in bound volumes (e.g., 12 issues of an annual serial be one or two volumes). Title and piece counts should not be considered the same as volume counts. If a volume count has not been kept, it may be estimated through sampling a representative group of title records and determining the corresponding number of volumes, then

extrapolating to the rest of the collection. As an alternative, an estimate may be made using the following formulae:

52 documents pieces per foot
10 "traditional" volumes per foot
5.2 documents pieces per volume

If either formulas or sampling are used for deriving your count, please indicate in a footnote.

Question 2c. Volumes Added. Include only volumes cataloged, classified, and made ready for use. Include government documents if they have been included in the count of volumes for Q. 1.

Question 4. Monographic Volumes Purchased. Report number of volumes purchased. Include all volumes for which an expenditure was made during 1994-95, including volumes paid for in advance but not received during the fiscal year. Include monographs in series and continuations. If only number of titles purchased can be reported, please report the data and provide an explanatory footnote in the "Footnotes" section of the questionnaire. **Note:** This question is concerned with volumes purchased rather than volumes received or cataloged. Question 16 requests the expenditure for the volumes counted here.

Questions 5-7. Serials. Report the total number of subscriptions, not titles. Include duplicate subscriptions and, to the extent possible, all government document serials even if housed in a separate documents collection. Verify the inclusion or exclusion of document serials in the footnotes section at the end questionnaire. Exclude monographic and publishers' series. A **serial** is:

a publication issued in successive parts, usually at regular intervals, and as a rule, intended to be continued indefinitely. Serials include periodicals, newspapers, annuals (reports, yearbooks, etc.), memoirs, proceedings, and transactions of societies.

Questions 6. Serials: Not Purchased. If separate counts of nonpurchased and purchased serials are not available, report only the total number of current serials received for Q. 7, and report **-1**, i.e. "U/A" for Q. 5 and Q. 6.

Question 8. Microforms. Report the total number of physical units: reels of microfilm, microcards, and microprint and microfiche sheets. Include all government documents in microform; footnote in the "Footnotes" section of the questionnaire if documents are excluded.

Question 9. Government documents. Report the total number of physical units (pieces) of government documents in paper format that have NOT been counted elsewhere. Include local, state, national, and international documents; include documents purchased from a commercial source if shelved with separate documents collections and not counted previously. Include serials and monographs. To estimate pieces from a measurement of linear feet, use the formula *1 foot = 52 pieces* and indicate in a footnote that the count is based on this estimate. Exclude microforms and nonprint formats such as maps or CD-ROMS.

Question 10. Computer files. Include the number of pieces of computer-readable disks, tapes, CD-ROMS, and similar machine-readable files comprising data or programs that are **locally held as part of the library's collections** available to library clients. Examples are U.S. Census data tapes, sample research software, locally-mounted databases, and reference tools on CD-ROM, tape, or disk. Exclude bibliographic records used to manage the collection (i.e., the library's own catalog in machine-readable form), library system software, and microcomputer software used only by the library staff.

Question 11. Manuscripts and archives. Included both manuscripts and archives measured in linear feet.

Question 12. Cartographic materials. Include the number of pieces of two- and three-dimensional maps and globes. Include satellite and aerial photographs and images.

Question 13. Graphic materials. Include the number of pieces of prints, pictures, photographs, postcards, slides, transparencies, film strips, and the like.

Question 14. Audio materials. Include the number of pieces of audio cassettes, phonodiscs, audio compact discs, reel-to-reel tapes, and other sound recordings.

Question 15. Film and video materials. Include the number of pieces of motion pictures, video cassettes, video laser discs, and similar visual materials.

Questions 16-27. Expenditures. Report all expenditures of funds that come to the library from the regular institutional budget, and from sources such as research grants, special projects, gifts and endowments, and fees for service. (For Q. 25 include non-library funds; see instruction Q. 24-25.) Do not report encumbrances of funds that have not yet been expended. **Canadian libraries should report expenditures in Canadian dollars.** (To determine figures in U.S. dollars, divide Canadian dollar amounts by 1.3794, the average monthly noon exchange rate published in the Bank of Canada *Review* for the period July 1994-June 1995.) **Please round figures to the nearest dollar.**

Question 16. Monographs. Report expenditures for volumes reported for Q. 4.

Question 17. Current Serials. Exclude monographs and publishers' series, and encumbrances.

Question 18. Other library materials. Include all materials except monographs and current serials, e.g. microforms, backfiles of serials, charts and maps, audiovisual materials, manuscripts, electronic media, etc. If expenditures for these materials are included in Q. 16 and/or Q. 17 and cannot be disaggregated, please report **-1**, i.e. "U/A" and provide a footnote in the "Footnotes" section of the questionnaire. Do not include encumbrances.

Question 19. Miscellaneous expenditures. Include any other materials funds expenditures not included in Q. 16-18, e.g., expenditures for bibliographic utilities, literature searching, security devices, memberships for the purposes of publications, etc. Please list categories, with amounts, in a footnote in the "Footnotes" section of the questionnaire. **Note:** if your library does not use materials funds for non-materials expenditures -- i.e., such expenditures are included in "Other Operating Expenditures" -- **report 0, not -1,** i.e. "U/A", for Q. 19.

Question 21. Contract binding. Include only contract expenditures for binding done outside the library. If all binding is done in-house, state this fact and give in-house expenditures in a footnote in the "Footnotes" section of the questionnaire; do not include personnel expenditures.

Question 22-25. Salaries and wages. Exclude fringe benefits. If professional and nonprofessional salaries cannot be separated, enter **-1**, i.e. "U/A" for Q. 22 and Q. 23 and enter total staff and enter total staff salaries as part of total salaries reported for Q. 25.

Questions 24-25. Salaries and wages: Student Assistants. Report 100% of student wages regardless of budgetary source of funds. Include federal and local funds for work study students.

Question 26. Other operating expenditures. Exclude expenditures for buildings, maintenance, and fringe benefits.

Question 28-31. Personnel. Report the number of staff in filled positions, or positions that are only temporarily vacant. Temporarily vacant positions are those positions that were vacated during the fiscal year for which ACRL data were submitted, and for which there is a firm intent to refill. You should only report positions for which there are expenditures for salaries reported for Q. 22-25.

Include cost recovery positions and staff hired for special projects and grants, but provide an explanatory footnote indicating the number of such staff. If such staff cannot be included, provide a footnote in the "Footnotes" section of the questionnaire. To compute full-time equivalents of part-time employees and student assistants, take the total number of hours worked by the part-time employees in each category and divide it by the number of hours considered by the reporting library to be a full-time work week. **Round figures to the nearest whole number.**

Question 28. Professional staff. Since the criteria for determining professional status vary among libraries, there is no attempt to define the term "professional." Each library should report those staff members it considers professional, including, when appropriate, staff who are not librarians in the strict sense of the term, for example, computer experts, systems analysts, or budget officers.

Question 30. Student Assistants. Report the total FTE (see instruction Q. 28-31) of student assistants employed on an hourly basis whose wages are paid from funds under library control or from a budget other than the library's, including federal work-study programs. Exclude maintenance and custodial staff.

Questions 32-33. Instruction. Sampling based on a typical week may be used to extrapolate TO A FULL YEAR for Q. 32 and Q. 33. Please use a footnote to indicate if responses are based on sampling.

Question 32. Presentations to Groups. Report the total number of sessions during the year of presentations made as part of formal bibliographic instruction programs and through other planned class presentations, orientation sessions, and tours. If the library sponsors multi-session or credit courses that meet several times over the course of a semester, each session should be counted. Presentations to groups may be for either bibliographic instruction, cultural, recreational, or educational purposes. Presentations both on and off the premises should be included as long as they are sponsored by the library. Do not include meetings sponsored by other groups using library meeting rooms. Place a footnote at the end of the questionnaire if you use sampling.

Questions 33. Participants in Group Presentations. Report the total number of participants in the presentations reported for Q. 32. For multi-session classes with a constant enrollment, count each person only once. Personal one-to-one instruction in the use of sources would be counted as reference transactions for Q. 34. Place a footnote at the end of the questionnaire if you use sampling. Use the "Footnotes" section to describe any special situations.

Question 34. Reference Transactions. Report the total number of reference transactions. A reference transaction is:

> *an information contact that involves the knowledge, use, recommendations, interpretation, or instruction in the use of one or more information sources by a member of the library staff. Information sources include printed and non-printed*

> *materials, machine-readable databases (including computer-assisted instruction), catalogs and other holding, records and, through communication or referral, other libraries and institutions, and persons both inside and outside the library.*

Include information and referral services. If a contact includes both reference and directional services, it should be reported as one reference transaction. When a staff member utilizes information gained from a previous use of information sources to answer a question, report as a reference transaction, even if the source is not consulted again during this transaction. Duration should not be an element in determining whether a transaction is a reference transaction. Sampling based on a typical week may be used to extrapolate TO A FULL YEAR for Q. 34. Place a footnote at the end of the questionnaire if you use sampling.

EXCLUDE SIMPLE DIRECTIONAL QUESTIONS. A directional transaction is an information contact that facilitates the logistical use of the library and that does not involve the knowledge, use, recommendations, interpretation, or instruction in the use of any information sources other than those that describe the library, such as schedules, floor plans, and handbooks.

Questions 35-37. Circulation. For Q. 35, count the number of initial circulations during the fiscal year from the general collection for use usually (although not always) outside the library. <u>Do not count renewals</u>. Include circulations to and from remote storage facilities for library users (i.e., do <u>not</u> include transactions reflecting transfers or stages of technical processing). Count the total number of items lent, not the number of borrowers. For Q. 36, report total circulation for the fiscal year including initial transactions reported for Q. 35 and renewal transactions. For both Q. 35 and Q. 36, exclude reserve circulations; report those for Q. 37.

Question 37. Reserve Circulation. Count the number of circulation transactions from the reserve collection. Count the total number of items, not the number of borrowers. Exclude circulations from other restricted-circulation collections, such as special collections. The reserve collection is defined as:

> *those materials that have been removed from the general library collection and set aside in a library so that they will be on hand for a certain course of study or activity in process. Usually, the circulations and length of loan of items in a reserve collection are restricted so that these items will be available to many users who have need of them within a limited time period.*

Questions 38-39. Interlibrary loans. Report the number of filled requests for material provided to other libraries for Q. 38. Report the number of filled requests for material received from other libraries <u>or document delivery services</u> for Q. 39. For both questions, include originals, photocopies, and materials sent by telefacsimile or other forms of electronic transmission. Do not include transactions between libraries covered by this questionnaire.

Questions 40-41. Ph.D. Degrees. Report the number awarded during the 1994-95 fiscal year. Please note that only the number of <u>Ph.D.</u> degrees are to be counted. Statistics on all other advanced degrees (e.g., D.Ed., D.P.A., M.D., J.D.) are not included in this survey. If you are unable to provide a figure for Ph.D.s only, please add a footnote in the "Footnotes" section of the questionnaire.

Question 41. Ph.D. Fields. For the purposes of this report, Ph.D. fields are defined as the specific specialties enumerated in the U.S. Department of Education's Integrated Postsecondary Education Data System (IPEDS) "Completions" Survey. Although the IPEDS form requests figures for all doctoral degrees, only fields in which <u>Ph.D.s</u> are awarded should be reported on the ACRL questionnaire. Any exceptions should be footnoted in the "Footnotes" section of the questionnaire.

Question 42. Instructional Faculty. Instructional faculty are defined by the U.S. Dept. of Education as:

> *Those members of the instruction/research staff who are employed full-time as defined by the institution, including faculty with released time for research and faculty on sabbatical leave. Full-time counts exclude faculty who are employed to teach fewer than two semesters, three quarters, two trimesters, or two four-month sessions; replacements for faculty on sabbatical leave or leave without pay; faculty for preclinical and clinical medicine; faculty who are donating their services; faculty who are members of military organizations and paid on a different pay scale from civilian employees; academic officers, whose primary duties are administrative; and graduate students who assist in the instruction of courses.*

Please be sure the number reported, and the basis for counting, are consistent with those for ACRL 1992-93 (unless in previous years faculty were counted who should have been excluded according to the above definition). Please footnote any discrepancies.

Questions 43-46. Enrollment. U.S. libraries should use the Fall 1994 enrollment figures reported to the Department of Education on the form entitled "Integrated Postsecondary Education Data System (IPEDS), Fall Enrollment 1994." The line and column numbers on the IPEDS form for each category are noted on the questionnaire. Please check these figures against the enrollment figures reported to ACRL in 1992-93 to ensure consistency and accuracy. **Note:** In the past, the number of part-time students reported was FTE; the number now reported to IPEDS is a head count of part-time students. Canadian libraries should note that the category "graduate students" as reported here includes all post-baccalaureate students.

Footnotes. Reporting libraries are urged to record in the footnote section any information that would clarify the figures submitted, e.g., the inclusion of branch campus libraries (see paragraph six of the "General Instructions" for definition of branch campus libraries). These explanatory footnotes will be included with the published statistics.

Supplementary to the questionnaire is a form where you may evaluate the electronic survey. We request that you complete the evaluation so that we might better address your concerns in coming years. Please return it with your ACRL program diskette.

Return the completed ACRL program diskette to the Library Research Center (LRC) office at the University of Illinois by **December 15, 1995**. If there are any questions about the procedure to be followed in completing this questionnaire, contact Diane LaBarbera at the LRC office at (217) 333-1980.

Please return your diskette and evaluation in the diskette mailer in which it arrived. Send all completed diskettes/questionnaires and evaluations to:

The Library Research Center
Library and Information Science Building
501 East Daniel Street
Champaign, IL 61820-6212

FOOTNOTES TO THE ACRL STATISTICS, 1994-95

Institution	Question No.	Notes
Akron	1	Includes government documents.
	30	1992-93 did not include work study.
	52	Includes Science Library.
	53	Includes Wayne College Library.
Alabama, Birmingham		Includes Lister Hill Library of the Health Sciences, Mervyn H. Sterne Library, and Nicolson Library - UAB Walker College.
Alaska	25	Six percent of total salaries were funded by special projects and grants; staff and student assistant hours were increased accordingly.
	53	Excludes Bristol Bay Campus (Dillingham), Kuskokwim Campus (Bethel), Northwest Campus (Nome), and Chukchi Campus (Kotzebue).
		Computing and Communications Department was reorganized and merged into Rasmuson Library in August 1994. Budget is $988,373 with 7 professional staff and 2 support staff. FY95 data for expenditures, personnel and instruction reported in this questionnaire reflects this change.
American		All figures are as of April 30, 1995.
	52	Includes Music Library.
	13	1992-93 figure revised to 297.
Andrews	14	1992-93 figures were inaccurate.
	52	Includes Architecture Resource Center and Music Materials Center branch libraries.
Arkansas, Fayetteville	52	Includes Physics Library, Fine Arts Library, Chemistry Library, and Learning Resource Center.
Atlanta		The Robert W. Woodruff Library serves five (5) institutions in the Atlanta University Center Consortium. They are: Clark Atlanta University (Graduate and Undergraduate); Interdenominational Theological Center (five denominational seminaries offering graduate degrees); Morehouse College (Undergraduate/Male); Morris Brown College (Undergraduate/Coed); Spelman College (Undergraduate/Female).
Ball State	7	Does not include depository document serials or other serials not purchased. FY95 count is a title count.
	9	Estimate assuming that 10% of the government publication collection is uncataloged.
	13	Excludes pieces of dioramas (2), games (60,668) kits (71,358), models (4,206), realia (59,070), and toys (683).
Baylor	1	All figures are as of May 31, 1995.
	52	Excludes Armstrong Browning Library, Baylor Collection of Political Materials, Dawson Church/State Center, School of Education Learning Resources Center, Strecker Museum, and Texas Collection (branch libraries).
	53	Includes Learning Resources Center, Baylor School of Nursing, Dallas campus.
Biola	1, 3	Physical count in 1995 is reflected in both 1994 and 1995 volume counts. Major weeding and adjustment of previous errors.
	7	1992-93 figure included continuations. 1992-93 figure revised to 896.

Institution	Question No.	Notes
Bowling Green State	4	Title count
	14	Largest collection of popular music in the U.S. outside of the Library of Congress. 1992-93 reporting revised to 1/2 million (estimate). Reporting abilities improved by better accounting capabilities.
	52	Includes Career Resource Center, Curriculum Resource Center, Music Library and Sound Recordings Archives, Popular Culture Library, and Science Library.
	53	Includes Firelands Campus.
Brandeis	7	This figure is a new tabulation of the serials received by the Brandeis Libraries.
	21	One time increase due to some supplemental funds.
Calgary		All figures are as of March 31, 1995.
	52	Includes Management Resource Centre and Gallagher Library of Geology and Geophysics.
Calif. Institute of Tech.		All figures are as of September 30, 1995.
Calif., Santa Cruz	19	Document delivery
Carnegie-Mellon	5	Includes documents serials.
	10	CD-ROM (5 jukeboxes, 200/per)
	12	Reporting of zero (0) in 1992-93 was incorrect.
	26	Excludes maintenance contract expenditures of $58,844 for library equipment.
	52	Excludes Hunt Institute for Botanical Documentation and Software Engineering Institute Library.
Catholic	1-3, 5-7	Includes Law Library statistics
Central Florida	12-15	Bibliographic units (not physical)
	34	Estimated from a typical week (1259/typical week x 50 weeks).
	52	Includes Curriculum Materials Center.
Claremont	19	Includes electronic resources, access services, OCLC Tech Pro, internal recurring payment (not all included in Misc. category in 1992-93).
	43-46	Compiled by controllers' office.
	48	Does not include all government documents serials.
	53	Includes Denison Library (Scripps College); Seeley G. Mudd Science Library (Pomona College); and Sprague Library (Harvey Mudd College).
	9	Government documents could not be disaggregated from "Volumes held..." categories in 1992-93
	18	Excludes electronic databases and access services
Clark		All figures are as of May 31, 1995.
	8	Estimate
	11	Estimate
Clemson	4	Title count
	7	Includes government docoments - previously not reported.
	6	Previously not reported.
	8, 10	Decrease in microform and increase in computer files due to changes in Government Printing Office format.
	14	Increase due to increased purchasing and processing of backlog of audio format

Institution	Question No.	Notes
Colorado, Denver	1	Formula used to determine number of government documents volumes.
	19	Document delivery services
	34	Sampling used to extrapolate total.
	40-46	Auraria Library serves the University of Colorado at Dever (UCD), Metropolitan State College of Denver (a 4-year institution), and the Community College of Denver. PhD degrees are awarded by UCD only. Faculty from all three institutions are reflected in 43 and 44. 44 and 46 reflect UCD enrollements only.
Colorado School of Mines	1, 2, 3	Decrease in collection due to massive weeding process.
	8	1992-93 was a title count. 1994-95 is a unit count.
	9	Used U.S. Document formula. Used Colorado State formula in 1992-93.
	10	Increase due to an increase in computer capabilities in library.
	13-14	Discontinued Graphic and Audio Collections.
	24, 30	Student FTE is an estimate. Salary figures include all wages paid.
	30	Estimate based on headcount and average hours worked.
	43-46	IPEDS data unavailable; data obtained from Registrar's Report.
Denver	6	Excludes non-purchased and U.S. Government serials.
	8	Excludes U.S. Governement depository microforms.
	9	Includes microforms.
	10	Increase attributable to U.S. Depository receipts.
	18	First year to acquire video laser disc materials.
	22	Excludes non-appointed professional staff ($5,307).
	26	Increase in ILS-related expenses (consortium expense and electronic filer).
	36	Includes some reserve circulation for Music Library branch.
	53	Includes Music Library branch (on a separate campus)
DePaul	18	All formats are accounted for in either the monograph or serial budgets.
	34	Based on actual and sampling data.
	53	Includes Chicago campuses (Lincoln Park and Loop) and Suburban campuses (O'Hare, Oak Brook, and South).
Drake		All figures are as of May 31, 1995.
	5	Excludes government documents.
Duquesne	1, 3	Decrease in holdings due to reclassification projects and weeding process.
	13	Previously not reported.
	14	Increase due to more 33 1/2 records.
	19	Increase from 1992-93 due to automation project (temporary increase).
	23	Reclassification project required extra part-time help.
East Texas State		All figures are as of August 31, 1995.
	15	Media Center is no longer included as it technically was never part of the Library.
	19	Computer sevices and Amigos charges. Should have been reported in 1992-93, but were not.
	53	Circulation and interlibrary loan statistics include the East Texas State University Metroplex Commuter Facility.

Institution	Question No.	Notes
Florida Atlantic	4	Includes firm order titles only. Not a volume count. Does not include approval.
	8	Excludes Documents, Davie, and North Palm Beach Libraries.
	16, 18, 19	Significant changes between 1992-93 and 1994-95 due to reallocation of resources budget.
	53	Includes Davie, Palm Beach Gardens, Fort Pierce, Fort Lauderdale (excludes contract with Broward County Public Library).
Fordham	52	Includes branch libraries in the Bronx, Manhattan and Tarrytown, NY.
George Mason	53	Includes Arlington Library Campus, Prince William Library, and Law Library.
George Washington	22, 28	Includes consultants (3052 consultant hours).
	26, 27	Includes payment by University to WRLC.
	28	1 cost recovery
	29	3 cost recovery; 9 contract
	30	2 cost recovery
	34	Sampling used to determine count.
	35, 36	Doesn't include GLIS or ILL figures which have been reported in the past.
	38, 39	GLIS does not distinguish libraries from individuals.
	53	Includes Virginia Campus Library, a department of Gelman Library, located in Ashburn, Virginia.
	19	Expenditures by categories are Document Delivery ($56,886), Literature Searching ($24,694),and Bibliographic Utility ($151,318).
Georgia State	37	Reserve statistics unavailable due to program error during rebasing of software.
Hahnemann	8	Main library only
	16, 28, 29, 30	Increase due to merger off four campus libraries into one.
	18	Figures included in Miscellaneous (19).
	19	Includes total from 18.
	35	Renewals cannot be disaggregated by existing automated library software.
	52	We are a newly merged University with 4 separate campus libraries: University Library, Center City Campus; Florence A. Moore Library of Medicine, East Falls Campus/Henry Avenue; Eastern PA Psychiatric Institute Library, East Falls Campus/Henry Avenue; and Learning Resource Center, East Falls Campus/Queen Lane.
Hofstra	5-7	Some government documents included in count of current serials.
Idaho	53	Includes ISU Library Services Center, Idaho Falls, ID.
Indiana/Purdue, Indianapolis	53	Branch Campus Libraries information includes Herron Library.
Indiana State	16	Infusion of funds caused large increase from last reporting.
Kansas State	32, 33	The number of presentations reflects number of tours and participants. Excludes the other bibliographic instruction sessions.
	53	Branch libraries included are administered by KSU Center Library with all funding per main campus budget. Excludes Salina Branch campus library data. KSU-Salina operates from an independently allocated budget.
Lehigh	19	Reported differently in past years.
	44	Reported differently in past years. Includes document delivery and bibliographic utilities.

Institution	Question No.	Notes
Louisiana Tech	10	Increase due to files of government documents.
	37	Reserve statistics are included in circulation statistics.
Louisville	10	Titles.
	13	Estimate.
	26	Fringe Benefits included in "Other Operating Expenditures" ($813,722).
	45, 46	Professional students, full-time (1,858), part-time (5) are included in graduate student categories.
Loyola, Chicago	4	Titles, not volumes.
	42	1993-94 Statistics mistakenly included many part-time faculty.
	53	Includes Lewis Library, Science Library, Mallinckrodt Library, Rome Center Library, Law Library and Medical Library.
Maine, Orono	53	Includes Darling Center branch library.
Marquette	8	Includes first full year of receiving ERIC microfiche in Main Library. Microform counts includes Law Library.
	10	Estimate - not all computer files are cataloged.
	13	All of graphics collection was transferred to another university department.
	15	Additional video collections were transferred to the Main Library. Includes Law Library video collection.
	19	Machine readable datafiles, computer software, computer software maintenance and faculty one-time purchase expenditures.
Maryland, Baltimore Ct	19	Changes from 1992-93 result because figures were pulled out differently due to internal subcoding reestablishment.
Memphis State	52	Includes Music Branch Library, Chemistry Branch Library, Mathematics Branch Library, Earth Sciences Branch Library, Audiology and Speech Language Pathology Branch Library, and Learning Media Center.
Miami, Ohio	9	Now many titles on CD-ROM.
	18	Items previously included with books and/or serials are now itemized under Other Library Materials.
	26	Includes $747,866 in fringe benefits.
	40	1992-93 figure revised to 42.
	52	Includes Edgar W. King Library (main), Amos Music Library, Brill Science Library, Southwest Ohio Regional Depository, and Wertz Art/Architecture Library.
	53	Excludes the regional campus libraries Gardner-Harvey Library, Miami University-Middletown - Middletown; Ohio Rentschler Library; and Miami University-Hamilton - Hamilton, Ohio.
Mississippi		Earlier data reported for 1992-93 ACRL was before the migration from one ILS (integrated library system) to a new system. Currently reported ACRL numbers are thought to be accurate.
	12, 13	Excludes special collections counted in 1993.
	16	Inflated expenditures due to availability of one-time money.
	52	Includes Blues Archives (Music Library), Chemistry Library, Government Documents Library, and Pharmacy Library.
Missouri, Kansas City	19	Material funds were used for membership in the Center for Research Libraries and some interlibrary loan expenses for the Law Library.
	41	The multi-interdisplinary PhD incorporates an additional 23 fields.

Institution	Question No.	Notes
Missouri, Kansas City (con'd)	53	Statistics are for the University Libraries at the University of Missouri-Kansas. UMKC is a campus of the University of Missouri System.
Missouri, Rolla	4	Total number of new titles added.
	5	Estimate.
	6	Estimate.
	8	Estimate.
	9	Counted differently this year, which accounts for the large increase from 1992-93.
Missouri, St. Louis	19	Previously unable to report.
Montreal		All figures are as of May 31, 1995.
	18	Included in monographs.
	25	Includes money spent on automation.
Nevada, Reno	10	Increase due to large increases in federal government materials on CD-ROM.
	40, 41	Increase in PhDs in Arts and Science plus graduates from several new programs.
New Brunswick		All figures are as of April 30, 1995.
	4	Figure reflects monographic title count. Excludes monographs in series.
	7	Excludes free government documents.
	19	For preservation filming.
New Hampshire	6	The definition of "not purchased" has changed within the library.
	8	Excludes government documents microfilms.
	42	Bargaining Unit faculty only.
New Mexico State	8, 42	Under reported in previous years.
	12	Over reported in previous years.
New Orleans	4	Figure reflects title count.
New School	19	The New School is a member of a consortium with New York University and Cooper Union. Included in this total is the consortium fee paid to NYU.
	34	Sampling used to extrapolate to a full year (46 weeks).
	52	Includes Adam & Sophie Gimbel Design Library of the Parsons School of Design and the Harry Scherman Library of the Mannes College of Music.
North Carolina, Greensboro	5-7	Excludes documents serials.
	19	Includes $50,000 for bibliographic utility.
	35, 36	Renewals not tracked separately. In addition to figure given, there were 129,729 in-house charges.
North Dakota State	42	Excludes lecturers. They are academic staff, not faculty.
	4	Includes titles purchased only.
	6	Includes government documents serials.
North Texas		All figures are as of August 31, 1995.
	1, 3, 9	In 1994, the method of reporting was changed. In 1993, government documents were included in 1 and 3. After 1994, government documents were broken out separately.
	2c	Used to included government documents. Flat budgets and serials cost increase also helped to make this figure lower.

Institution	Question No.	Notes
North Texas (cont'd)	16	Budgets have been flat and serials costs have been rising, leading to reductions in the purchase of monographs.
	18	Now includes payments for data access (e.g. First Search).
	19	Incudes document delivery (not included in 1993).
	21	Decrease due to static budgets.
	34	Reference transactions interpolated from reported 7,000 in a typical week.
	42	Includes all faculty, part and full time.
	43-46	From "UNT Fact Book - 94/95 Edition."
Northeastern	17	Includes expenditures for Other Library Materials formats (microform, CD-ROM) received as, and counted as, subscriptions. Includes memberships for purposes of receiving publications.
	18	Excludes current serials subscriptions received in microform or CD-ROM formats and memberships for purposes of reeiving serial subscriptions.
	19	Includes cable TV access ($1,176), bibliographic utilities ($56,000), database access ($18,589), data communication lines ($31,489), and consortium dues ($26,465).
	53	Includes Burlington and Nahant (Marine Science Center).
Northern Arizona	1, 3, 9	1992-93 statistics were inaccurate for these questions.
	10	Proliferation of CD-ROMs and AIMED files.
	16	State increases funds 25% annually to cover rising subscription costs.
	38	Program has increased 60-70% each year.
	40	Expanded PhD program.
Northern Colorado	4	Excludes monographs in series.
	7	Excludes Government Publications. Includes monographs in series.
	12	Estimate.
	16	Excludes monographs in series.
	17	Includes monographs in series and memberships.
	52	Includes Music Library and Laboratory School Library.
Northern Illinois	4	Excludes Law Library.
	5	6,362 for Main Library, 3,072 for Law Library.
	53	Includes all branch libraries (Faraday Library, Hoffman Estates Education Center Library, Lorado Taft Campus Library, Map Library, Music Library, Law Library, Rockford Education Center Library).
Ohio	4-6	During 1994-95 we transitioned from the VTLS acquisitions subsystem to INNOVAC, making it impossible to compile accurate figures on the number of monographs or serials that were purchased, as opposed to received and cataloged.
	7	Includes government document serials.
	12-13	Main campus only
	19	Expenditures for bibliographic utilities, online searching fees, etc. are included as "Other operating expenditures" (26).
	24	Includes $373,050 regular and $213,789 in federal work-study funds.
	34	Sampling used to determine number of reference transactions at at Chillicothe, Lancaster, and Zanesville. Other based on actual counts.
	39	19,911 borrowed by all campuses, minus 4,143 intra-campus fills.
	52	Includes Music/Dance Library on Athens campus.

Institution	Question No.	Notes
Ohio (cont'd)	53	Includes main campus in Athens, as well as the five regional campuses in St. Clairsville (Eastern), Chillicothe, Lancaster, Ironton (Southern), and Zanesville.
Old Dominion	19	Includes computer files and search services ($14, 903) and document delivery/interlibrary loan ($4,030).
	34	Based on sampling
	40	Unable to provide number of PhDs awarded in 1994-95.
	52	Includes Hofheimer Art Library.
Ottawa	52	Includes Science Library and Main Library.
	53	Includes branch campus at Pembrooke, Hawkesbury, and Cornwall.
Pacific	13	Figure given for Special Collections photograph collection.
	14	Includes Lawton Harris Folkdance Collection.
	24	Includes wages from Library funds only.
	45	Includes 1st professional degree. New programs added, including MBA.
	46	Includes 1st professional degree.
	52	Includes Science Library.
Pepperdine	52	Includes Culver City Educational Center, Irvine Educational Center, Long Beach Educational Center, Encino Educational Center, and Westlake Village Educational Center.
Polytechnic	53	Includes Long Island Campus Library, Farmingdale, NY.
Portland State	19	Increase from last reporting due to separate reporting of consorita expenditures in this category.
Rhode Island	53	Includes College of Continuing Education Library, Providence Center Providence, RI.
	53	Includes Pell Marine Science Library, Graduate School of Oceanography, Bay Campus, Narragansett, RI.
SUNY Binghamton	18	Includes microforms, electronic media, and a/v materials.
	19	Includes utilities, memberships for electronic access, lit. searching. Excludes memberships for publications.
	35	Initial and renewal circulation figures cannot be disaggregated.
	52	Includes Science Library.
SUNY, Coll. Env. Sci. & For.	10	We have 4 CD-ROM databases which use 12 disks.
	32	Figure is based on 1 credit course (5 weeks meets 3x per week) 7 sections x 3 classes = 21 sessions a week.
	33	Total of 100 students are enrolled in these 7 sections.
	35	Can't give initial circulation only figure. Initial and renewal circulations are counted as one.
SUNY, Coll. Env. Sci. & For. (con'd)	53	There are two very small collections at remote sites in Adirondack Mts. We purchase and process materials for these collections but statistics volume count are not available.
San Diego State	30, 34	Based on the month of October.
	53	Excludes Imperial Valley Campus.

Institution	Question No.	Notes
San Francisco	12	Increase in cartographic holdings due to new acquisitions and better record keeping.
	14	Decrease in audio holdings due to discarded items (transferred to Media Center) and the new items (268) are mostly from the off-campus centers.
	15	New: mostly in off-campus centers.
	53	Includes Sacramento Regional Center Library and San Ramon Regional Center.
South Dakota	16, 19	Increases due to new fee money.
	45	Does not include medical or law students.
South Dakota State	5, 7	Includes periodical subscriptions only.
	10, 14	Includes materials not previously counted separately.
	16	Includes proceeds froma new student fee used to begin an approval plan.
	18	Includes expenditure for electronic resources (CD-Rom, etc.).
South Florida	53	1992-93 data reflected Tampa Campus only. 1994-95 data includes Tampa (Tampa Campus Library, Tampa Medical, and Florida Mental Health Institute), St. Petersburg, Sarasota, and Ft. Myers Campus Libraries.
Southern Methodist	1,3	All figures are as of May 31, 1995.
	4	Excludes Underwood Law Library.
	16, 17	Includes microform expenditures.
	18	Excludes microform expenditures.
	28	Includes three special projects staff.
	32, 33, 34	Includes Central University Libraries only.
	34	Estimate.
	36	Includes reserves.
	52	Includes totals for the three autonomous library units on campus: Central University Libraries (comprising Fondren Library, Science/Engineering Library, DeGolyer Library, Hamon Arts Library and Institute for the Study of Earth and Man Reading Room), Bridwell Theology Library, and Underwood Law Library.
Southern Mississippi	34	Based on typical fall week.
	52	Includes McCain Library and Archives and Teaching Learning Resource Center.
	53	Excludes Branch campus at Gulf Park.
Southwestern Louisiana	52	Includes Education Library.
St. John's	53	Includes Loretto Memorial Library, Staten Island, NY.
	21	We have no contract, per se, to spend a specific amount or bind a particular number of volumes with a specific binder.
St. Louis	53	Includes Parks College Library.
Stevens Inst. of Tech.	7	Library also has direct access to Engineering Information collection of about 2,500 titles.
	19	Includes Online services ($22,000), OCLC ($14,148), ILL ($27,400), memberships ($2,525), and deposit accounts ($3,000).
Teachers College		All figures are as of April 30, 1995.
	34	Figure based on typical week: 1925 X 44 weeks.

Institution	Question No.	Notes
Teachers College (cont'd)	37	Reserve automated August 1994. Statistics cover August 1994 through April 30, 1995.
	40-42	Information supplied by Office of Institutional Studies.
	43-46	Teachers College is a graduate institution.
Tennessee Tech	16	Amount expended, not amount expended for volumes (volumes as noted in 4) as this number (4) is unavailable.
Texas, Arlington		All figures are as of August 31, 1995.
	4	Excludes count of monographs in series and continuations .
	7	Includes count of memberships and plans.
	16	Includes backfiles of serials.
	19	Only memberships and plans for purposes of publications. Figures could not be disaggregated in previous reportings.
	24	Excludes federal work-study funds.
	34	Sampling: 2529/typical week x 50 weeks.
	42	1992-93 faculty included some adjuncts who were not included in 1994-95.
	52	Includes Architecture and Fine Arts and Science and Engineering Libraries.
Texas, Dallas		All figures are as of August 31, 1995.
	53	Includes GIL, Callier, Corporate Information Services.
Texas Woman's	19	Includes Bibliographic Utilities ($71,086), Preservation ($71,678), Document Delivery ($2,945), Software/Hardware Maintenance ($112,404), A-V Hardware ($45,000), and Diary ($5,000).
	34	Based on typical week..
Toledo	5	Includes a limited number of government documents.
	53	Includes Scott Park Learning Resource Center.
Tulsa		All figures are as of May 31, 1995.
	4	Excludes Law Library.
	6	Includes GPO subscriptions.
	22	Excludes the Law Library Director's salary. (He is on the Law School faculty.)
U.S. International	8	No longer use three ERIC fiche machines.
	53	Includes USIU - Mexico City, USIU - Nairobi, and USIU - Orange County Center.
Utah State	2a	Includes 32,000 recently converted and not previously reported volumes
	2b	Re-classication of Sci-tech monographs revealed physical volume count lower than historical bibliographic count and 18,267 volumes have been removed from the statistics for this collection (counted as withdrawals).
	4	Lost approval program; now buying discount books.
	9	Decrease due to increase in machine readable records.
	15	Expunged 16mm films from collection causing a substantial drop in Film and Video holdings.
	34	New branch libraries created a need for larger staff.
	41	Ended combination of PhD fields when University received Carnegie I status.
	46	Increased cost of tuition, changes in Utah's definition of part time students, and an increase in international graduate students accounts for growth in this category.
	53	Includes The Moore Library,The Educational Resources & Technology Center, and the Quinney Natural Resources Library (branch libraries).

Institution	Question No.	Notes
Vermont	6	Includes monographic series.
		Unit count excludes U.S. government documents serials.
	8	Count of microform units excludes U.S. government documents microforms.
	34	Extrapolated from Fall semester week plus Dana Medical Library statistics.
	52	Includes Dana Medical Library and Cook Chemistry/Physics Library.
Virginia Commonwealth		All personnel and budget figures exclude numbers associated with media staff (artists, camera technicians, etc.) reporting to the library.
	21	Includes contract and in-house binding.
	28	Includes 2.65 grant-funded FTE.
	30	Includes 2.4 grant-funded FTE .
Wake Forest	52	Includes the Worrell Professional Center library on the main campus.
	53	Includes the Coy Carpenter Library of medical school.
Wichita State	19	Fees paid to cooperative organizations ($72,092) .
	52	Includes Chemistry Library and Music Library.
William and Mary	11	Manuscripts not included previously.
	43-46	Figures are for fall 1995.
	52	Includes Geology, Biology, Music, Physics, and Chemistry Libraries.
	53	Includes Virginia Institute of Marine Science, Gloucester Point, Virginia.
Windsor		All figures are as of April 30, 1995.
	36	Includes Reserve Room statistics.
	43-46	FFTE (fiscal full-time equivalent)
	52	Includes Paul Martin Law library.
Wisconsin, Milwaukee	9	Includes uncataloged government documents and microforms.
	34	Figures are from sampling.
	43, 44	Includes undergraduates and graduate students.
Wyoming	4, 16	Because of diversion of money to buy serials, less is available for books.
	13, 14	1992-93 revised to N/A (Not Applicable to library).
	53	Includes Midtown Campus - Hedi Steinberg Library at Stern College for Women, Brookdale Campus - Dr. Lillian and Dr. Rebecca Chutick Law Library at the Benjamin N. Cardozo School of Law, and Jack and Pearl Resnick Campus - D. Samuel Gottesman Library at the Albert Einstein College of Medicine.

NAMES AND LOCATIONS OF PARTICIPATING INSTITUTIONS: 1994-95

Institution	Full Name of Institution	Location
Akron	University of Akron	Akron, Ohio
Alabama, Birmingham	University of Alabama, Birmingham	Birmingham, Alabama
Alaska	University of Alaska, Fairbanks	Fairbanks, Alaska
American	American University	Washington, D.C.
Andrews	Andrews University	Berrien Springs, Michigan
Arkansas, Fayetteville	University of Arkansas, Fayetteville	Fayetteville, Arkansas
Atlanta	Atlanta University Center	Atlanta, Georgia
Ball State	Ball State University	Muncie, Indiana
Baylor	Baylor University	Waco, Texas
Biola	Biola University	La Mirada, California
Bowling Green State	Bowling Green State University	Bowling Green, Ohio
Brandeis	Brandeis University	Waltham, Massachusetts
Calgary	University of Calgary	Calgary, Alberta
Calif. Institute of Tech.	California Institute of Technology	Pasadena, California
Calif., Santa Cruz	University of California, Santa Cruz	Santa Cruz, California
Carnegie-Mellon	Carnegie-Mellon University	Pittsburgh, Pennsylvania
Catholic	Catholic University of America	Washington, D.C.
Central Florida	University of Central Florida	Orlando, Florida
Claremont	Claremont Colleges	Claremont, California
Clark	Clark University	Worcester, Massachusetts
Clarkson	Clarkson University	Potsdam, New York
Clemson	Clemson University	Clemson, South Carolina
Cleveland State	Cleveland State University	Cleveland, Ohio
Colorado, Denver	University of Colorado, Denver	Denver, Colorado
Colorado School of Mines	Colorado School of Mines	Golden, Colorado
Denver	University of Denver	Denver, Colorado
DePaul	DePaul University	Chicago, Illinois
Drake	Drake University	Des Moines, Iowa
Duquesne	Duquesne University	Pittsburgh, Pennsylvania
East Texas State	East Texas State University	Commerce, Texas
Florida Atlantic	Florida Atlantic University	Boca Raton, Florida
Fordham	Fordham University	Bronx, New York
George Mason	George Mason University	Fairfax, Virginia
George Washington	George Washington University	Washington, D.C.
Georgia State	Georgia State University	Atlanta, Georgia
Hahnemann	Medical College of Pennsylvania & Hahnemann University	Philadelphia, Pennsylvania
Hofsta	Hofstra University	Hempstead, New York
Idaho	University of Idaho	Moscow, Idaho
Idaho State	Idaho State University	Pocatello, Idaho
Illinois State	Illinois State University	Normal, Illinois
Indiana/Purdue, Indianapolis	Indiana University-Purdue University (IUPUI)	Indianapolis, Indiana
Indiana State	Indiana State University	Terre Haute, Indiana
Kansas State	Kansas State University	Manhattan, Kansas
LaSierra	LaSierra University	Riverside, California
Lehigh	Lehigh University	Bethlehem, Pennsylvania
Louisiana Tech	Louisiana Tech University	Ruston, Louisiana
Louisville	University of Louisville	Louisville, Kentucky
Loyola, Chicago	Loyola University Chicago	Chicago, Illinois
Maine, Orono	University of Maine, Orono	Orono, Maine
Marquette	Marquette University	Milwaukee, Wisconsin
Maryland, Baltimore Ct.	University of Maryland Baltimore County	Baltimore, Maryland
Memphis State	Memphis State University	Memphis, Tennessee
Miami, Ohio	Miami University	Oxford, Ohio
Michigan Technological	Michigan Technological University	Houghton, Michigan
Mississippi	University of Mississippi	University, Mississippi
Missouri, Kansas City	University of Missouri, Kansas City	Kansas City, Missouri
Missouri, Rolla	University of Missouri, Rolla	Rolla, Missouri

NAMES AND LOCATIONS OF PARTICIPATING INSTITUTIONS: 1994-95

Institution	Full Name of Institution	Location
Missouri, St. Louis	Unversity of Missouri, St. Louis	St. Louis, Missouri
Montana State	Montana State University	Bozeman, Montana
Montreal	University of Montreal	Montreal, Quebec
Nevada, Reno	University of Nevada, Reno	Reno, Nevada
New Brunswick	University of New Brunswick	Fredericton, New Brunswick
New Hampshire	University of New Hampshire	Durham, New Hampshire
New Mexico State	New Mexico State University	Las Cruces, New Mexico
New Orleans	University of New Orleans	New Orleans, Louisiana
New School	New School for Social Research	New York, New York
North Carolina, Greensboro	University of North Carolina, Greensboro	Greensboro, North Carolina
North Dakota State	North Dakota State University	Fargo, North Dakota
North Texas	University of North Texas	Denton, Texas
Northeastern	Northeastern University	Boston, Massachusetts
Northern Arizona	Northern Arizona University	Flagstaff, Arizona
Northern Colorado	University of Northern Colorada	Greeley, Colorado
Northern Illinois	Northern Illinois University	DeKalb, Illinios
Old Dominion	Old Dominion University	Norfold, Virginia
Ohio	Ohio University	Athens, Ohio
Pacific	University of the Pacific	Stockton, California
Pepperdine	Pepperdine University	Malibu, California
Polytechnic	Polytechnic University	Brooklyn, New York
Portland State	Portland State University	Portland, Oregon
Puerto Rico	University of Puerto Rico	Rio Piedras, Puerto Rico
Rhode Island	University of Rhode Island	Kingston, Rhode Island
Rockefeller	Rockefeller University	New York, New York
SUNY, Binghamton	Binghamton University, State University of New York	Binghamton, New York
SUNY Coll. of Env. Sci. & For.	State Univ. of NY, College of Environ. Science and Forestry	Syracuse, New York
San Diego State	San Diego State University	San Diego, California
South Florida	University of South Florida	Tampa, Florida
San Francisco	University of San Francisco	San Francisco, California
South Dakota	University of South Dakota	Vermillion, South Dakota
South Dakota State	South Dakota State University	Brookings, South Dakota
Southern Methodist	Southern Methodist University	Dallas, Texas
Southern Mississippi	University of Southern Mississippi	Hattiesburg, Mississippi
Southwestern Louisiana	University of Southwestern Louisiana	Lafayette, Louisiana
St. John's	St. John's University	Jamaica, New York
St. Louis	St. Louis University	St. Louis, Missouri
Stevens Inst. of Tech.	Stevens Institute of Technology	Hoboken, New Jersey
Teachers College	Teachers College - Columbia University	New York, New York
Tennessee Tech	Tennessee Technological University	Cookeville, Tennessee
Texas, Arlington	University of Texas, Arlington	Arlington, Texas
Texas, Dallas	University of Texas, Dallas	Dallas, Texas
Texas Woman's	Texas Woman's University	Denton, Texas
Toledo	University of Toledo	Toledo, Ohio
Tufts	Tufts University	Medford, Massachusetts
Tulsa	University of Tulsa	Tulsa, Oklahoma
U.S. International	United States International University	San Diego, California
Utah State	Utah State University	Logan, Utah
Vermont	University of Vermont	Burlington, Vermont
Virginia Commonwealth	Virginia Commonwealth University	Richmond, Virginia
Wake Forest	Wake Forest University	Winston-Salem, North Carolina
Wichita State	Wichita State University	Wichita, Kansas
William and Mary	College of William and Mary	Williamsburg, Virginia
Windsor	University of Windsor	Windsor, Ontario
Wisconsin, Milwaukee	University of Wisconin, Milwaukee	Milwaukee, Wisconisn
Wyoming	University of Wyoming	Laramie, Wyoming
Yeshiva	Yeshiva University	New York, New York